CAMBRIDGE

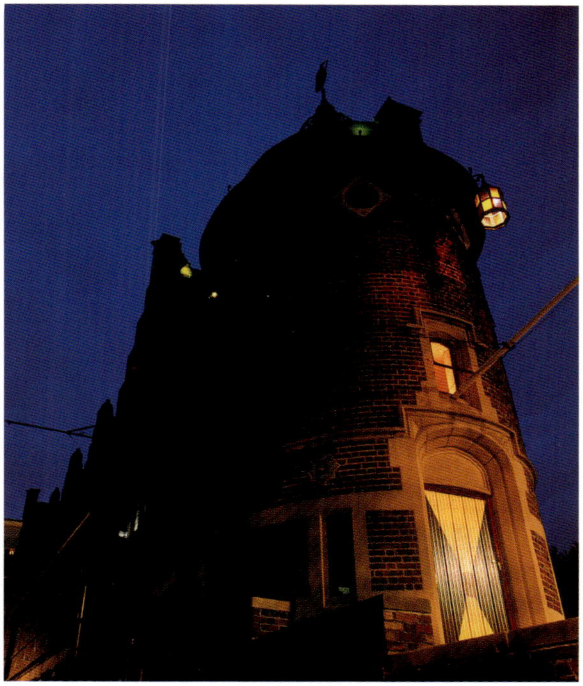

Portrait of a Restaurant

CAMBRIDGE

GALEN SATURLEY

Blue Tree
PORTSMOUTH

First published in the United States in 2005
by Blue Tree, LLC.
P.O. Box 148
Portsmouth, NH 03802
www.TheBlueTree.com

37 10 1

First Edition

Production editor: Elizabeth Antalek

Printed in Hong Kong

Library of Congress
Cataloging-in-Publication Data

Saturley, Galen.
Cambridge / Galen Saturley
Includes index.
1. Cambridge I. Title
2007930863

ISBN-10: 0-9792014-1-1
ISBN-13: 978-0-9792014-1-7

For customer service and orders:
Local 603.436.0831
Toll-Free 1.866.852.5357
Email sales@TheBlueTree.com

Blue Tree
AN ARTISTIC PUBLISHING COMPANY

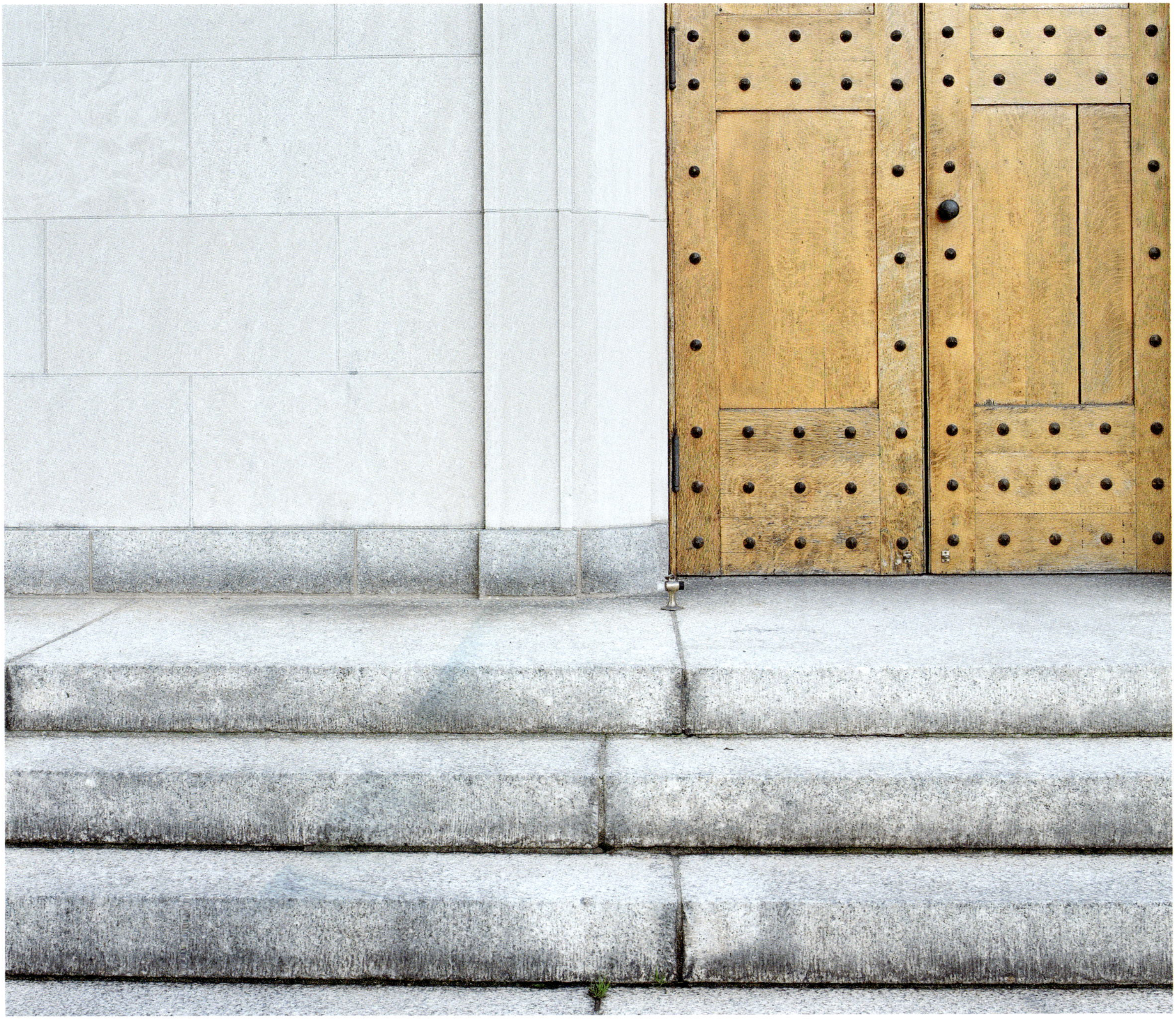

For my wife, Liza

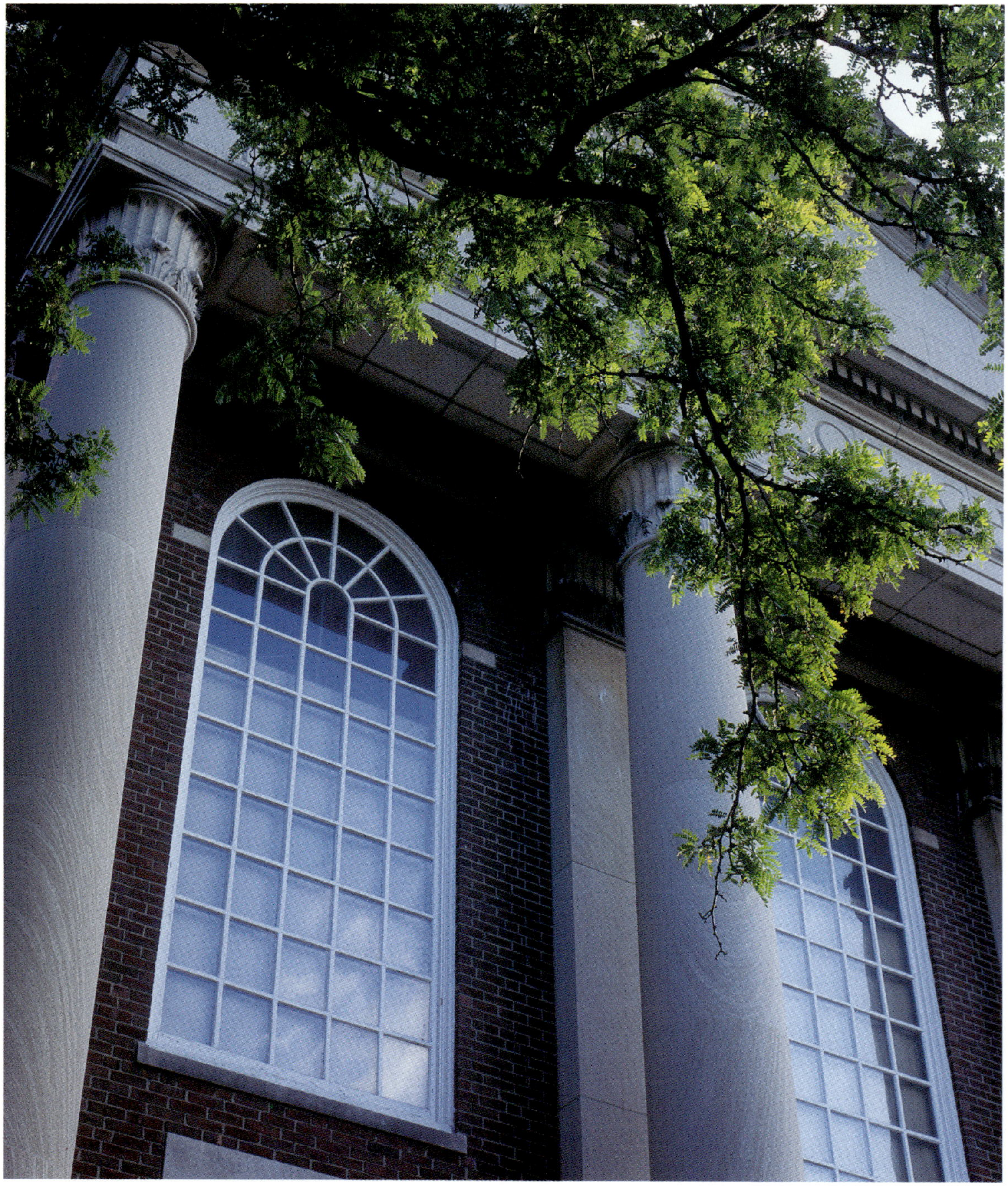

Servio Garcia
Camilo Diaz

Paul O'Connell
Bob Cina
Tim Morrill

Tony Maws
Marjorie Maws

Nicole Coady

Dylan Black
Pete Sueltenfuss

Keith Pooler

Larry Burdick
Paula Burdick
Cathy Watson

Rachel Klein
Catherine Dry

Gabriel Bremer
Analia Verolo
Francisco Salmeron

Raymond Ost
Gwen Trost

Tim Wiechmann
Bronwyn Wiechmann

Tom Berry
Rudy Maniscalco

Nick Zappia
Jorge Lopes

Gerard Lopez

Mary-Catherine Deibel
Deborah Hughes
Steven Brand

Casablanca
Chez Henri
Craigie Street Bistrot
Finale
Green Street
Harvest
L.A. Burdick
OM Restaurant
Rialto
Salts Restaurant
Sandrine's Bistro
T.W. Foods
Temple Bar
The Blue Room
The Elephant Walk
Upstairs on the Square

chapter one

Spring

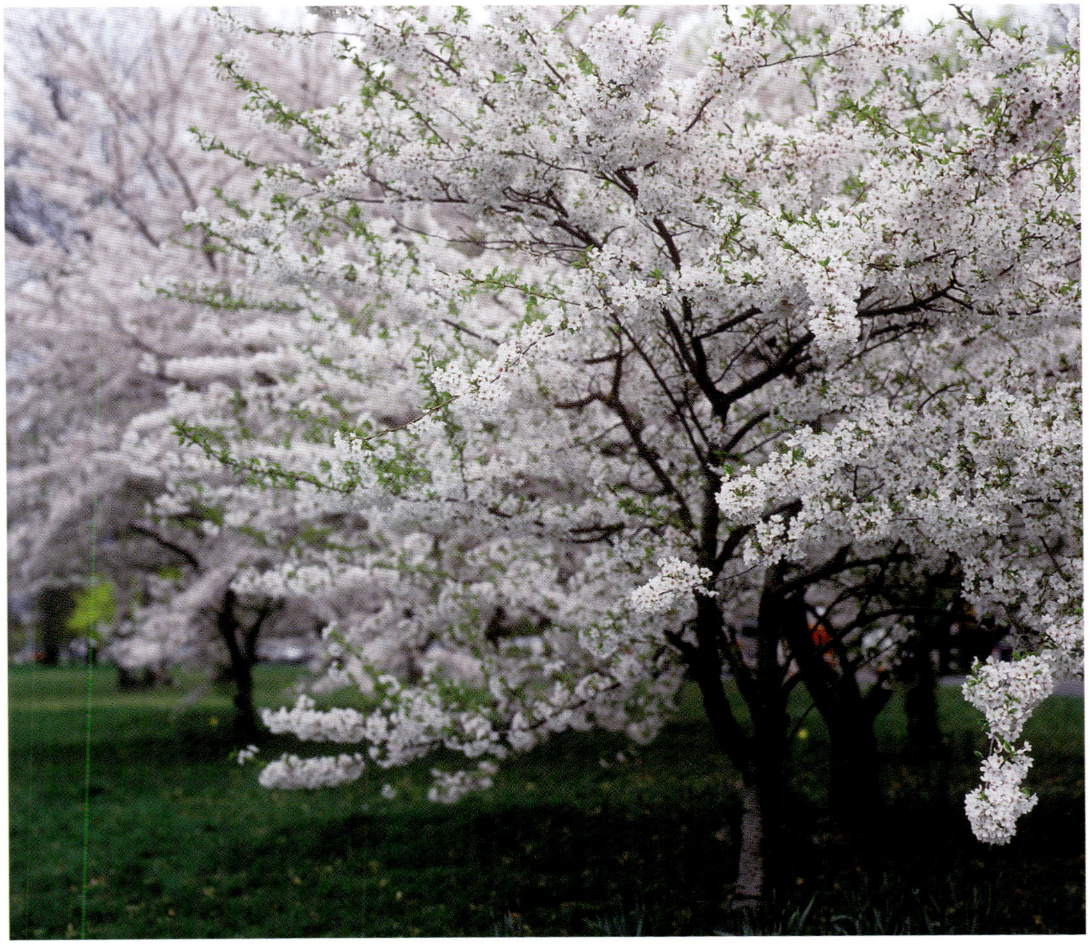

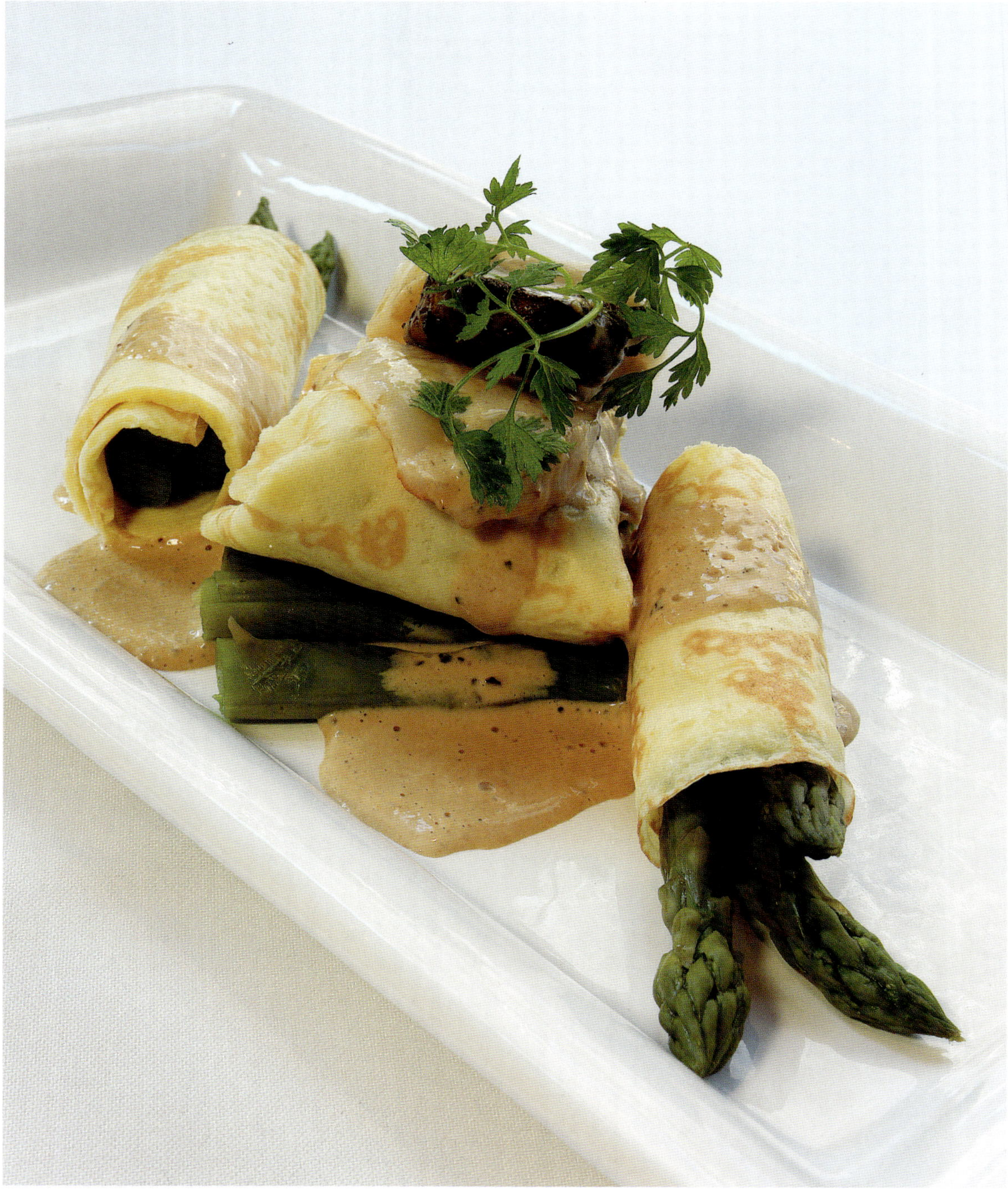

Scallop and Foie Gras-Stuffed Crêpes

Crêpe Batter

½ quart milk
1½ cups flour
3 eggs
salt to taste
4 tablespoons melted butter

Stuffing for Crêpes

12 U-10 Scallops, pan-seared on each side
½ pound fresh foie gras, cut in 1½-ounce slices and pan-seared on both sides in an extremely hot pan
18 stalks asparagus, blanched
1 bunch chives, chopped finely

Champagne Beurre Blanc

6 ounces shallots, finely minced
1 bottle dry Champagne
½ ounce champagne vinegar
½ quart heavy cream
1 ounce black peppercorns, crushed
sea salt to taste
½ pound unsalted butter

Serves 6

Put the flour, salt, and eggs in a bowl and slowly add the milk, gently stirring with a balloon whisk until the batter is smooth. Add the melted butter and whisk until the butter has absorbed the batter. Strain the batter through a sieve or chinois. Let the dough rest for 2 hours, covered, in the refrigerator.

Cook Crêpes

Heat an 8-inch Teflon crêpe or sauté pan over medium-high heat—350° to 375°. Warm ½ teaspoon canola oil or clarified butter in the pan. Pour in a 1-ounce ladle of batter. Spread evenly in the pan by swirling the pan over the heat. Cook crêpes 1-2 minutes on each side. Make 2 crêpes per person.

Champagne Beurre Blanc

Sauté shallots until golden with 1 teaspoon of butter. Deglaze with Champagne and champagne vinegar, then add black pepper, heavy cream, and salt. Reduce by ⅔, then whisk butter into the reduction about a tablespoon at a time. Add more butter if the sauce is not emulsified; it should have the consistency of heavy cream. Season to taste. Keep warm.

Finishing the Dish

Lay the crêpe flat on a plate. In the middle of the crêpe, put 1 scallop (sliced horizontally) and top with a slice of pan-seared foie gras. Fold the crêpe in half and repeat with another. Arrange on a plate the two stuffed crêpes and 2 asparagus cut in half; warm the plate in the oven for 5 minutes at 325°. When hot, nap the crêpes with sauce and garnish with chopped chives. Serve immediately.

Roasted Escolar and Grilled Hawaiian Blue Prawn

Escolar

2 ¼ pounds escolar—6-ounce portions per person
¼ cup grapeseed oil
3 tablespoons lemon juice
2 tablespoons unsalted butter
kosher salt
cracked white pepper

Blue Prawns

6 prawns, shells removed but heads and tails left attached
3 cloves garlic, shaved
2 tablespoons grapeseed oil
kosher salt
cracked black pepper

Chili Mayonnaise

1 cup mayonnaise
2 teaspoons sugar
½ teaspoon chili powder
½ teaspoon cayenne powder
1 teaspoon siracha
1 teaspoon Korean chili oil
zest one lemon
kosher salt too taste

Basil Puree

1 bun basil
1 cup baby spinach
½ clove garlic
salt to taste
olive oil
kosher to taste
sugar to taste

Baby Zucchini Salad

12 baby zucchini
12 cups rocket arugula
1 tablespoon lemon juice
1 tablespoon olive oil
salt
cracked black pepper

Serves 6

Served with Rocket Arugula, Baby Zucchini, Basil Puree, and Chili Mayonnaise

In a stainless steel sauté pan, bring grapeseed oil up to medium-high heat. Cook fish on all sides until golden-brown and cooked medium. Add lemon juice and butter. Baste fish until it develops a nice, shiny glaze. Remove from pan and let rest for 3-5 minutes. Slice and serve.

Blue Prawns

Mix oil and garlic together. Place shrimp in marinade and let sit for 3 hours. Season with salt and pepper. Grill shrimp until medium-rare or desired temperature.

Chili Mayonnaise

Mix all ingredients together with a whisk. Check salt seasoning.

Basil Purée

Blanch basil and spinach in boiling salted water for 30 seconds. shock in ice water and drain. Rough chop basil and spinach and squeeze out excess water. Place garlic and oil in blender a blend smooth. Place spinach and Basil in blender and puree with olive oil for one minute, or until bright green. Season too taste with salt and sugar.

Baby Zucchini Salad

Slice raw baby zucchini on mandolin, ⅛-inch thick. Toss the zucchini and arugula with the lemon and olive oil. Season with salt and pepper.

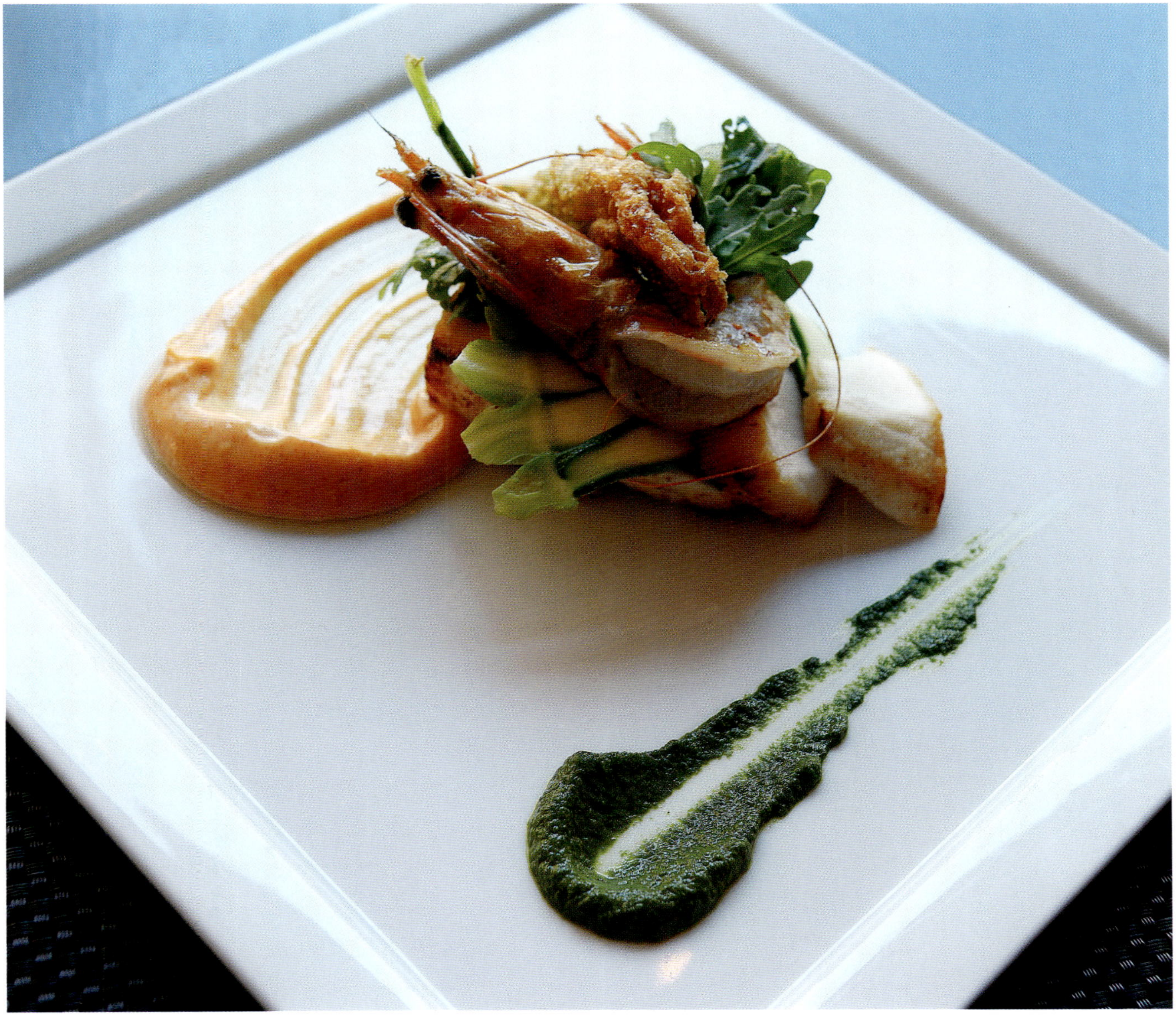

OM Restaurant

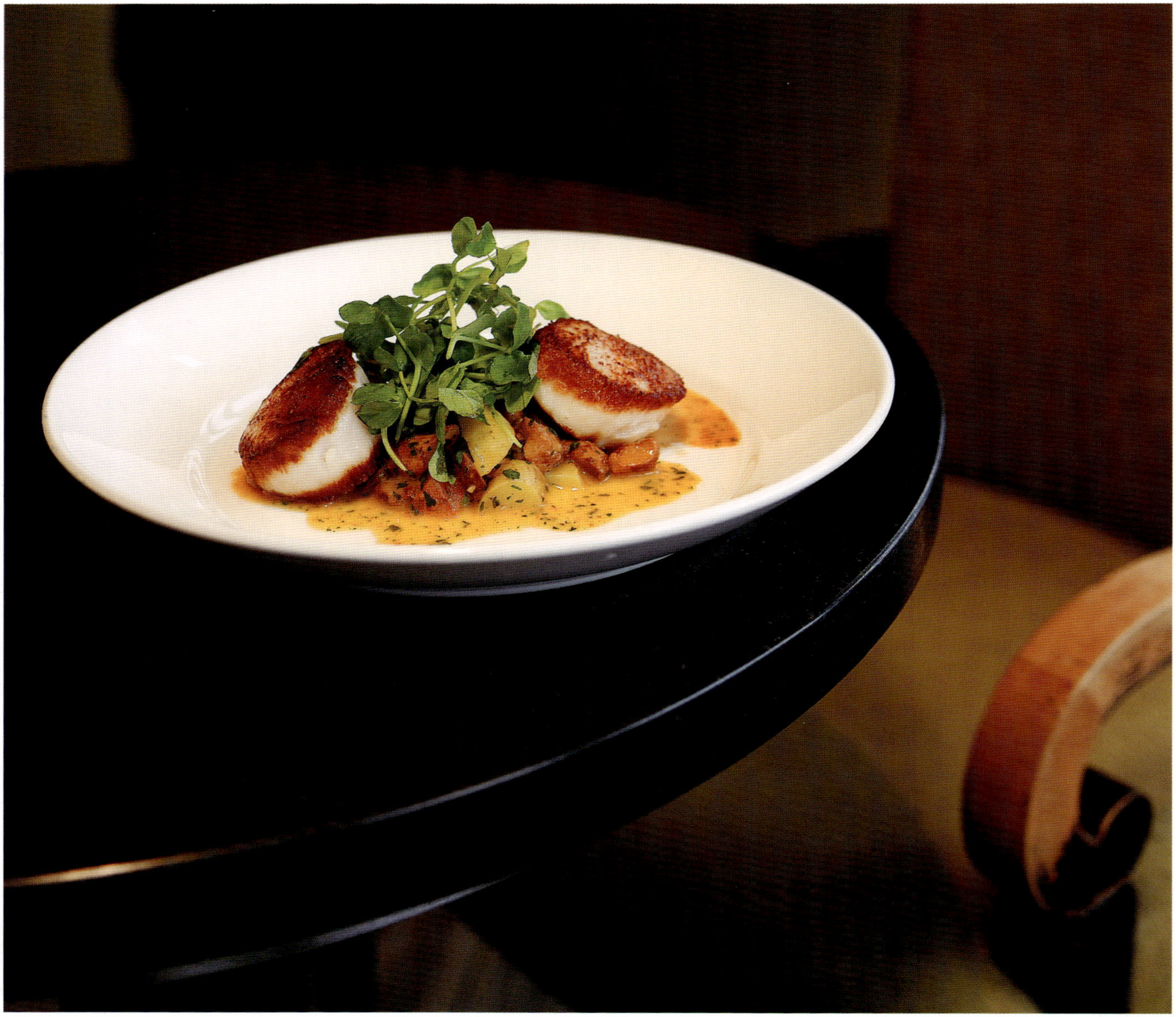

Seared Sea Scallops

Served with Citrus Beurre Noisette and Spring Potato Salad

Beurre Noisette

1 stick (4 ounces) unsalted butter
juice of 3 limes, 3 lemons, 2 oranges (should yield 8 ounces juice)
1 tablespoon Dijon mustard
½ shallot sliced
1 tablespoon sugar

Scallops

12 large U-10 Scallops
light olive oil for cooking

Spring Potato Salad

light olive oil for cooking
1 pound fingerling potatoes, boiled in salted water, chilled, and cut in halves lengthwise
1 cup sliced and washed leeks, sweated over low heat with olive oil and chilled
1 cup freshly shucked, blanched, and chilled English peas
½ cup citrus beurre noisette
2 cups baby pea tendrils or watercress for garnish

Serves 4

Scallops

Preheat a large skillet over medium-high heat. Season the scallops on both sides with salt and pepper. Coat the bottom of the skillet with olive oil and sear the scallops on each side until golden, about 2 minutes per side. Serve with citrus beurre noisette and spring potato salad.

Beurre Noisette

Gently brown the butter in a small pan over medium heat—approximately 10 minutes. While the butter is browning, add the juice, Dijon, shallot, and sugar to a blender and puree smooth. When the butter is lightly browned and nutty smelling, pour all at once into the juice mixture, being careful not to let it boil over. Season with salt and pepper and purée until emulsified.

Spring Potato Salad

Heat a large pan over high heat and coat the bottom lightly with olive oil. Add the potatoes and cook until lightly brown, about 3 minutes. Season with salt and pepper. Add the cooked leeks, peas, and citrus beurre noisette and continue cooking until hot, about one minute.

To Serve

Divide the potato salad on 4 plates. Arrange 3 scallops around each and drizzle the remaining citrus sauce on the plate. Garnish with the baby pea greens or watercress.

Peruvian Ceviche

12 ounces bay scallops, cleaned and rinsed
1 medium red onion, sliced very thin
2 ounces lime juice
2 ounces Meyer lemon juice
½ teaspoon garlic, ground
¼ cup ahi amarillo, minced
¼ cup cilantro, chopped
¼ cup parsley, chopped
2 ears corn, blanched and cut into 3 pieces each
butter lettuce for garnish
plantain chips for garnish

Serves 6

In Peru, fishermen will often place all of the ingredients for ceviche in a plastic bag, shake it up, and dine out of the bag. At Chez Henri we mix all of the ingredients in a chilled bowl and arrange them on a chilled plate.

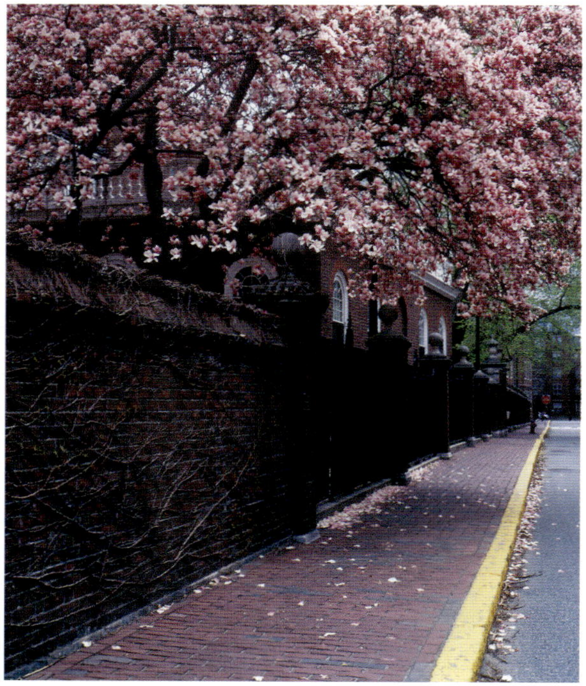

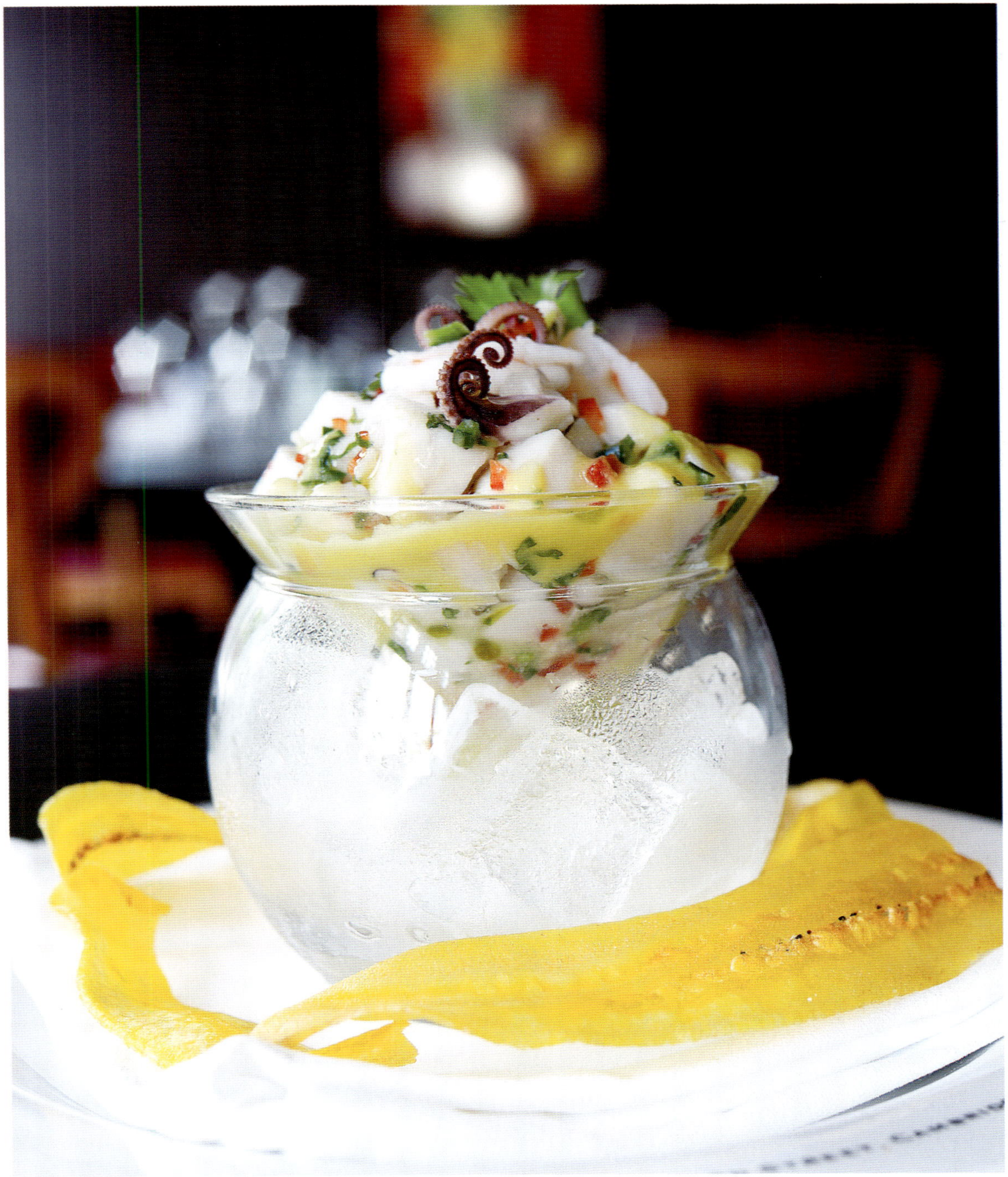

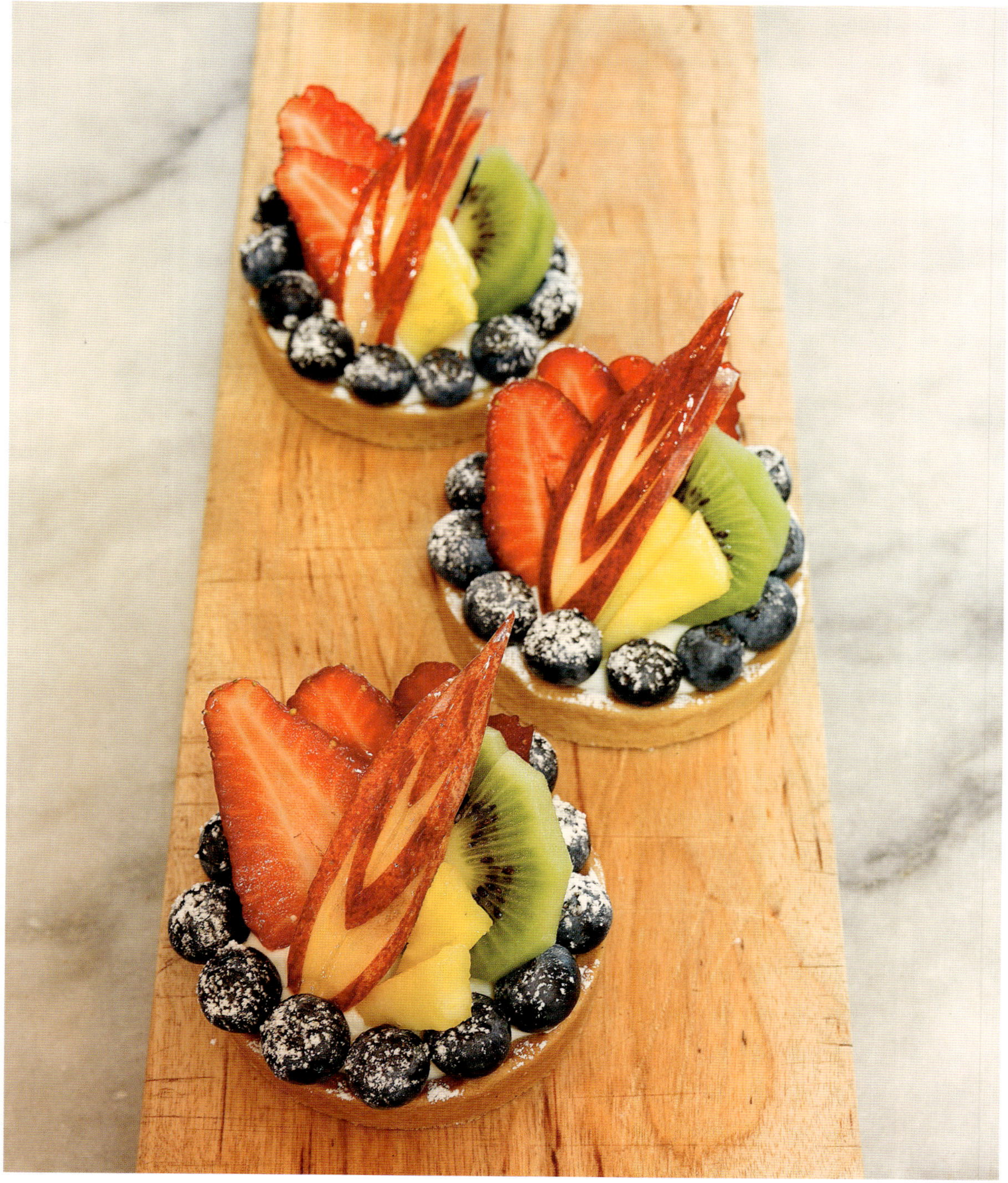

Fruit Tart

L.A. Burdick

Lemon Curd

2 lemons, juiced
zest of 1 lemon
2 eggs
⅓ cup sugar
2 tablespoons unsalted butter, softened

Dough

2 sticks unsalted butter
¾ cup sugar
pinch salt
½ vanilla bean
zest of 1 lemon
1 egg
2 ¼ cups flour
1¼ cups almond flour

high-quality chocolate

Lemon Curd

Combine lemon juice, zest, eggs, and sugar in a heavy-duty saucepan over medium heat, whisking constantly until thick. Strain and add softened butter, stirring until combined. Chill in the refrigerator overnight.

Dough

Cream butter, sugar, salt, vanilla bean, and zest. Add the egg and mix until thoroughly combined. Gradually add flour and almond flour and incorporate. Chill the dough in the refrigerator overnight.

Roll dough to ⅛-inch thickness and line a tart shell mold. Bake at 325° for 20 minutes or until golden-brown. Let cool.

Brush the bottom of the tart shell with melted chocolate. Whip 1 cup of heavy cream, fold under ½ cup lemon curd, spoon into the tart shell, and top with your choice of fresh fruit.

Avocat Kanthor

Dressing

2 garlic cloves, chopped
¼ cup shallots, chopped
¾ tablespoon galangal, chopped
2 tablespoons peanuts
5 teaspoons fish sauce
½ cup water
1½ tablespoons rice vinegar
1 tablespoon lime juice
1 tablespoon sugar
½ teaspoon salt
¼ teaspoon black pepper
¼ teaspoon red pepper flakes

Salad Ingredients

2 each, semi-ripe avocados
8 ounces fresh tuna, sushi grade
1 tablespoon lemongrass, finely minced
1 tablespoon shallots, finely minced
2 teaspoons French mint leaves, thinly sliced
2 teaspoons Asian basil, thinly sliced
baby greens for garnish, such as mache or mesclun
1-2 tomatoes, sliced

Serves 4

In a heavy skillet over medium-high heat, toast the garlic, shallots, and galangal, stirring often, until softened and lightly browned, 3 to 4 minutes. Put them in a blender with water and process, pulsing off and on, until well chopped, about 1 minute. Remove the mixture to a small bowl, add the peanuts and the remaining dressing ingredients, and mix well. Set aside.

Cut the tuna into ¾-inch cubes. Halve the avocado lengthwise and remove the seed. Being careful to keep the avocado flesh and skins intact, scoop out each half with a large spoon. Setting aside 12 slices, about ¼-inch thick, for garnish, cut the remaining avocado into cubes the same size as the tuna. In a large bowl, gently toss the tuna and avocado cubes with the lemongrass, shallots, mint, basil, and ¼ cup of the dressing. Spoon the mixture into the avocado skins.

On 4 individual plates, lay out some baby greens and place the stuffed avocado skins on top of the sliced tomatoes—1 avocado over 3 slices of tomato—and garnish with the avocado slices fanned out on the plate. Drizzle the remaining dressing lightly over the baby greens and avocado slices.

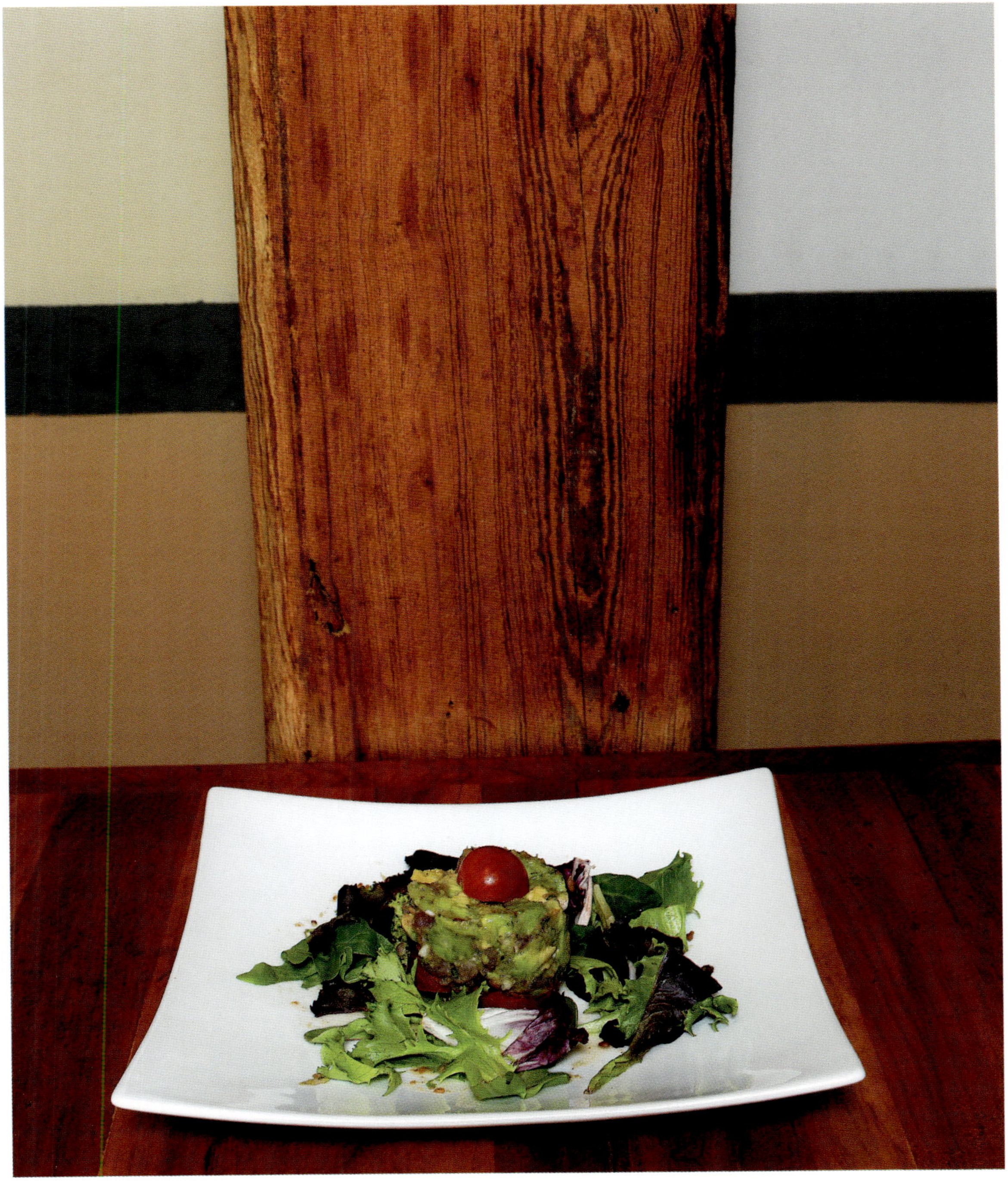

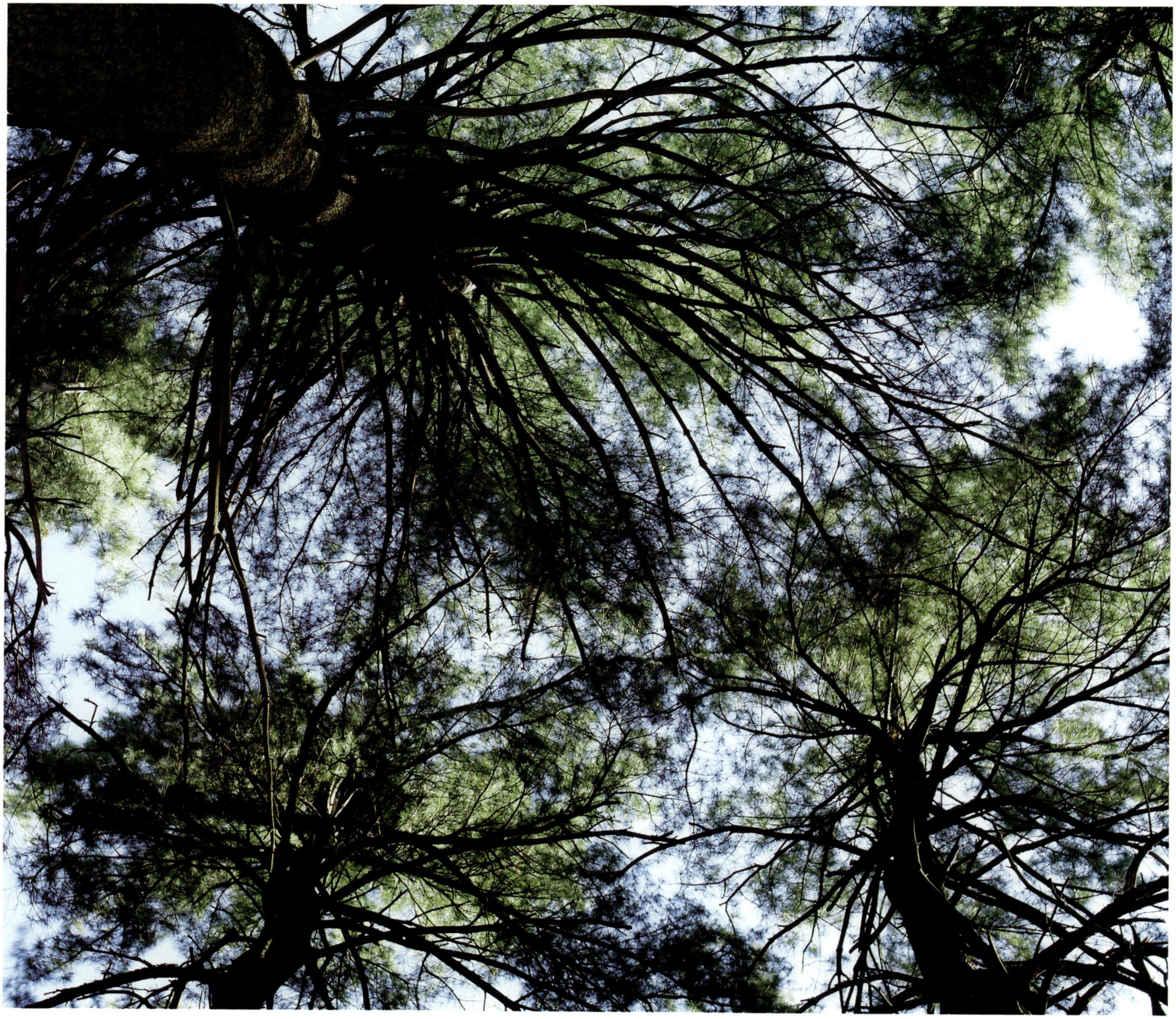

Spring Asparagus with Grapefruit

24 asparagus

unsalted butter
3 large grapefruit
grapefruit zest
1 shallot
2 egg yolks
6 ounces champagne vinegar
2 tablespoons water
salt and pepper

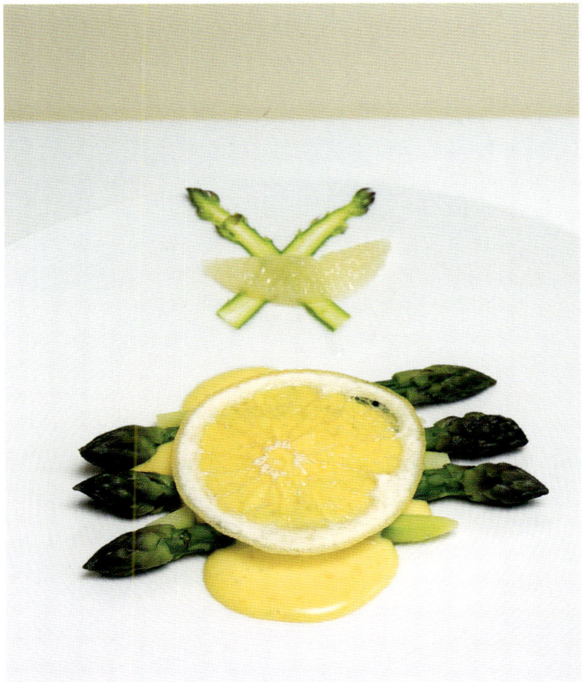

Grapefruit Sauce Maltaise

Clarify 8 ounces unsalted butter. Reduce juice of 1 grapefruit with vinegar and sliced shallot to almost dry. In a separate bowl, add the 2 egg yolks and 2 tablespoons of water and whisk over a double boiler until the mousse doubles in volume and comes away from the bottom of the pan. Slowly trickle in the clarified butter at an equal temperature. Fold in small dice of grapefruit zest that has been blanched 3 times in water. Keep warm.

Asparagus

Peel the stalks and with a small knife manicure the tips so they look perfect. Boil in salted water and drain. Place on the plate and cover with the sauce. Garnish with thinly sliced tips and grapefruit segments.

T.W. Food

Poached Sweetbreads

Poached Sweetbreads

1 pound, or lobe, sweetbreads
1 carrot
½ onion
1 garlic clove
2 sprigs thyme
6 black peppercorns
2 cloves
2 cups white wine
4 cups water

Hazelnut Vinaigrette

¼ cup rice wine vinegar
1 teaspoon Dijon mustard
2 tablespoons chopped hazelnuts
¼ cup extra-virgin olive oil
¼ cup hazelnut oil

Spring Mix of Green Vegetables

1 bunch asparagus
½ pound fava beans, shelled
¼ pound English peas, shelled
haricots verts
6 baby zucchini, washed and cut in half lengthwise
6 ramps, trimmed of "beard"
1 teaspoon canola oil
½ tablespoon butter

Preheat the oven to 325°.

Prepare the vinaigrette by first combining the hazelnuts, Dijon mustard, and rice wine vinegar and then slowly drizzling in the two oils in a steady stream with a whisk. Combine thoroughly and set aside. Do not refrigerate the vinaigrette; it should be at room temperature when you drizzle the warm plate with it at the end.

Place the carrot, onion, garlic, herbs, spices, and liquid in a nonreactive 8-ounce stockpot or pasta pot and bring to a boil. With a ladle, skim off any impurities that rise to the surface, then lower the heat to a simmer. Place the entire lobe of sweetbreads in the liquid and cover the pot with a kitchen towel (not a lid). Simmer for approximately 10 minutes for medium-rare to medium-temperature. Remove the sweetbreads from the pot and cover with the towel to retain moisture as they cool. When they're cool, peel any extra membrane or clumps of fat from the sweetbreads. Don't take too much off, though, or the sweetbreads will fall apart. Portion out about 4 ounces per person. Set aside in the refrigerator.

With the sweetbreads in the refrigerator, begin blanching the vegetables. They must be blanched separately. Begin with a salted pot of boiling water, blanch the asparagus for 3 minutes, then strain it out and shock in an ice bath. Using the same boiling water, blanch the fava beans for 5 minutes and shock, and then the haricots verts for 3 minutes and shock. Remove the shocked vegetables from their ice bath and set aside with the washed baby zucchini and the trimmed ramps.

Heat a sauté pan over medium-high heat and add the canola oil and butter to the pan. Season the sweetbreads with salt and pepper and place them in the pan to brown. When a nice crisp brown sear appears on one side, flip the sweetbreads over and do the same to the other side. Place them in the oven to keep them warm while the vegetables are prepared.

In another sauté pan, heat some olive oil and add all the green vegetables to the pan. Quickly sauté them until they're hot, approximately 3 minutes on medium-high heat. Arrange the vegetables on the bottom of a plate, making sure to get a good mixture, place a portion of sweetbreads on top, and drizzle the dish with the hazelnut vinaigrette (make sure to whisk it again before drizzling to remix the ingredients). Serve immediately.

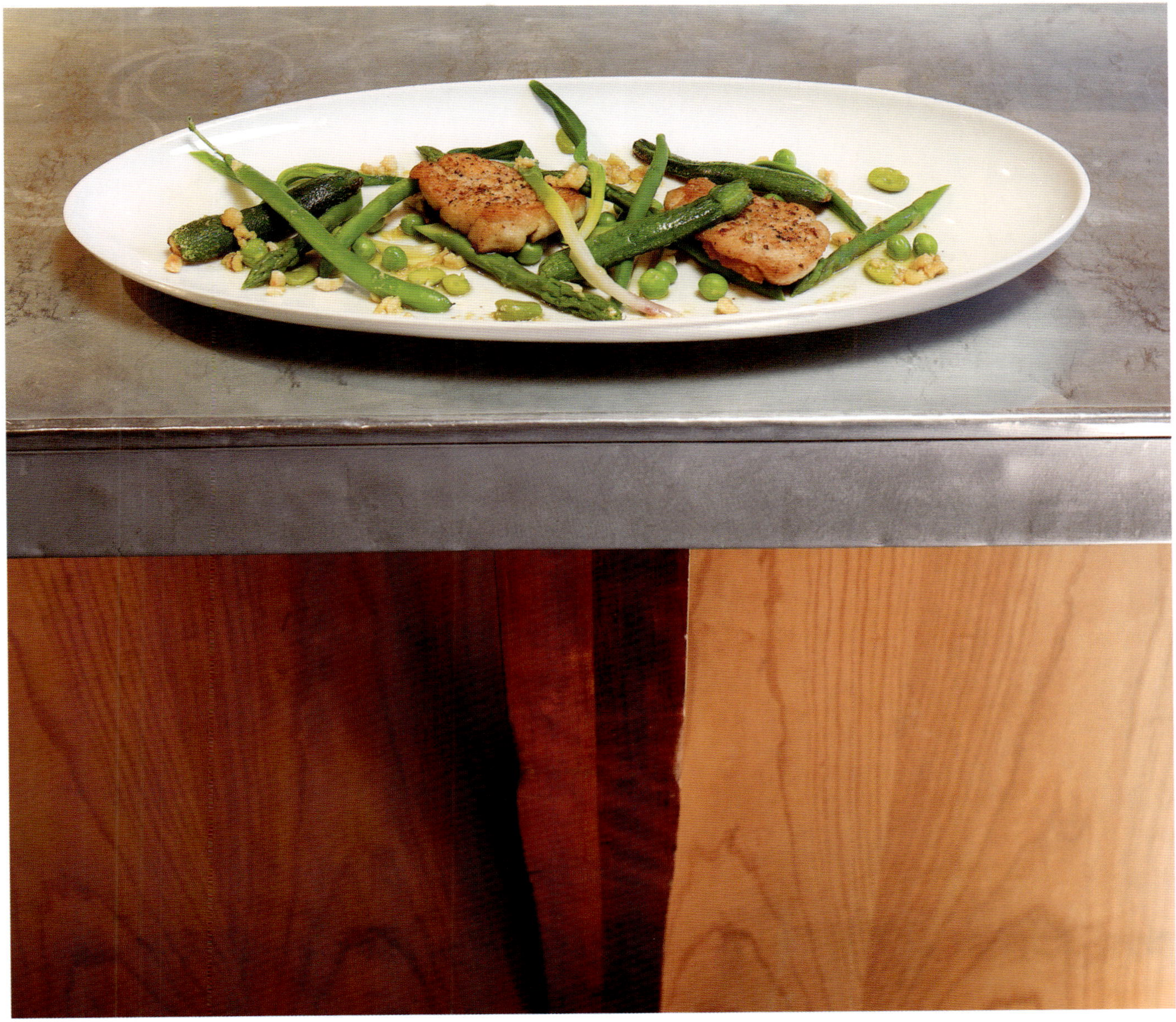

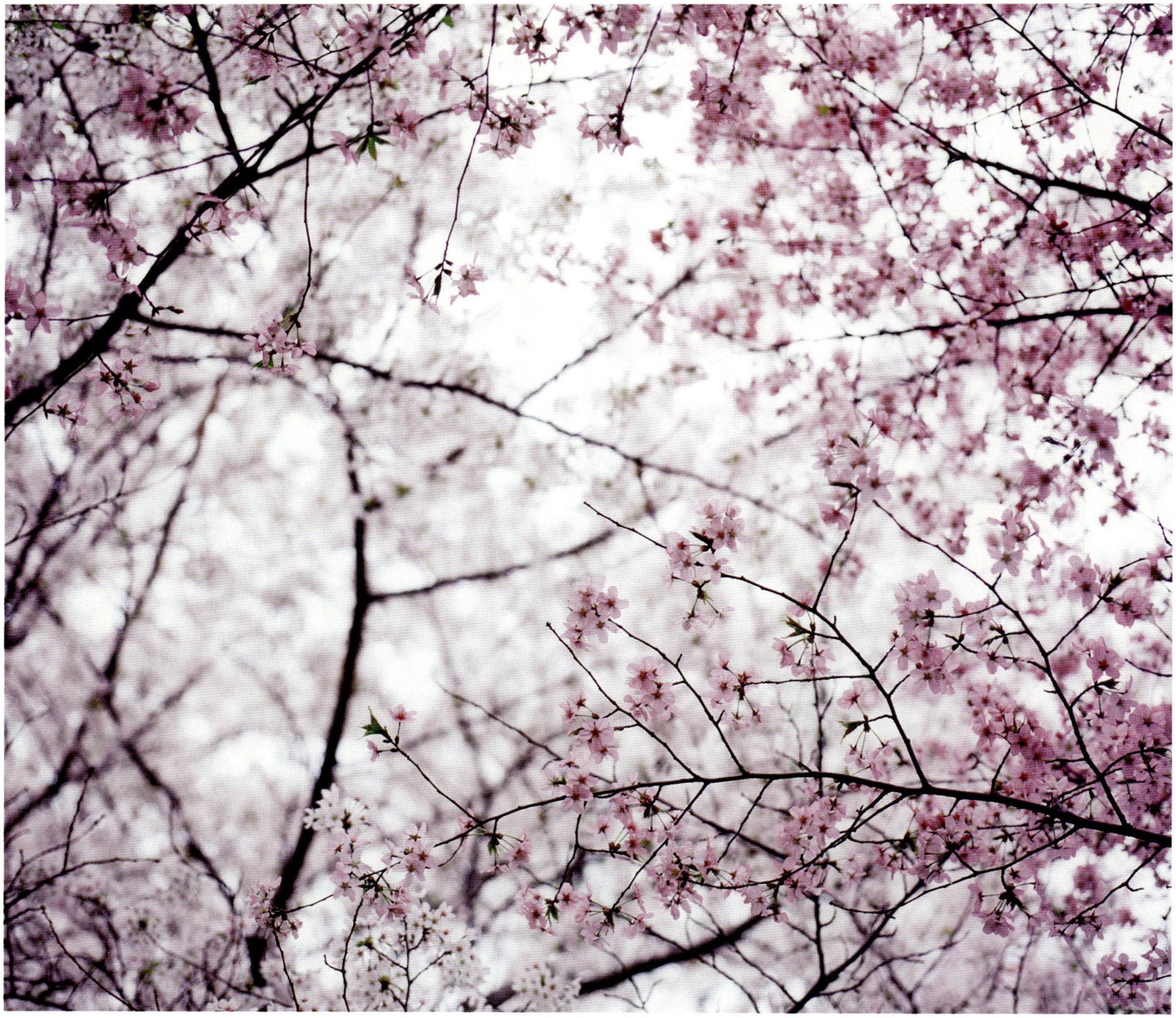

Roasted Saddle of Spring Lamb

1 lamb loin, trimmed
1 pound spring-dug parsnips
3 cups heavy cream
1 fresh bay leaf
4 shallots, diced
4 cloves of garlic, minced
1 tablespoon butter
1 cup Madeira wine
1 cup half & half
3 sprigs fresh rosemary
3 sprigs fresh thyme
4 large egg yolks
salt and pepper
½ loaf brioche, crust removed and diced small
6 spring onions
olive oil

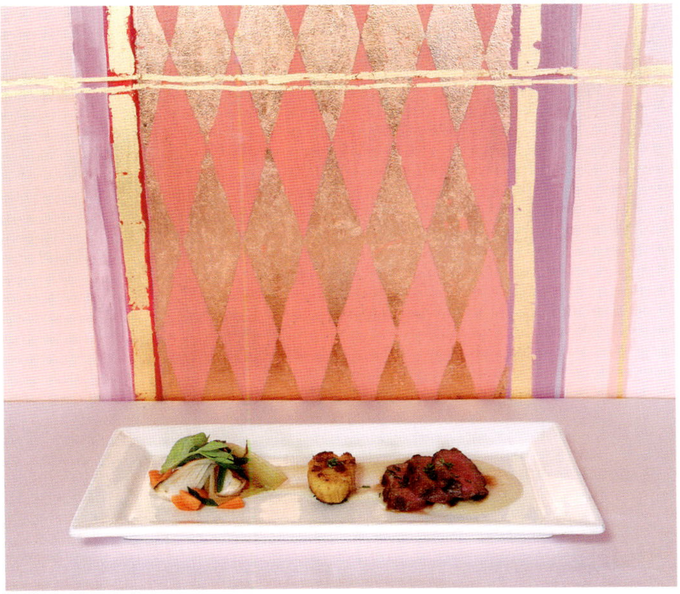

Served with Caramelized Bread Pudding and Early Spring Onions

Peel parsnips and chop roughly, place in a saucepot with 2 cups heavy cream and the bay leaf, and simmer on medium heat until tender. Strain the parsnips, reserving cooking liquid. Purée parsnips, adjusting consistency by adding reserved cooking liquid. Keep warm.

Sweat the shallots and garlic in butter, add wine, and reduce by half. Add 1 cup heavy cream and the half & half and bring to a simmer, then add thyme and rosemary. Remove from heat and let herbs infuse for 5 minutes, then strain. Place egg yolks in a metal bowl and whisk together, temper in cream mixture season, with salt and pepper, and add bread. Let bread absorb the liquid, then place in a baking dish and cover in aluminum foil. Bake in a water bath at 300° for 30 minutes.

Quarter the spring onions and toss with oil and salt and pepper and roast at 350° for 8 minutes or until tender.

Sear the lamb in a sauté pan over medium heat until most of the fat has rendered, 8-10 minutes, then place in a 350° oven for 6-8 minutes for medium doneness.

Eggs en Cocotte with Crab and Rock Shrimp

4 six-ounce ramekins
salt and pepper, to taste
8 eggs
1 pound green garlic tops
¼ cup sake
¼ pound honshimeji mushrooms
butter
1 teaspoon white miso
¼ pound crabmeat
⅛ pound fresh rock shrimp
Beurre monté
¼ teaspoon lemon juice
2 tablespoons chopped herbs, such as parsley, chives, tarragon, or chervil
piment d'espelette, or spicy Hungarian paprika
4 slices toast

Serves 4

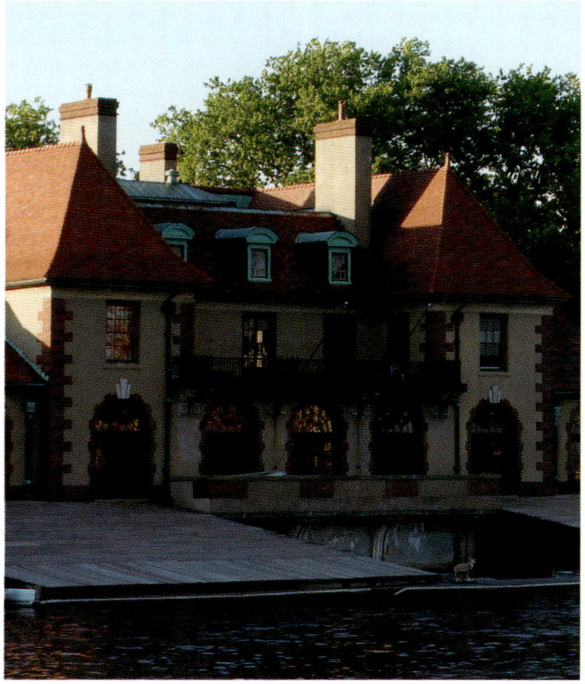

Preheat oven to 350°.

Butter 4 six-ounce ramekins and season them with salt and pepper. Crack 2 eggs into each ramekin and place in a water bath. Set aside.

Blanch green garlic tops in well-salted boiling water. When the garlic tops are tender, shock them immediately in ice water. Purée them in a blender with water and the sake until smooth. Pass through a chinois. Set aside.

Sauté the mushrooms in butter, and season with salt and pepper to taste. Add the miso, crab, shrimp and buerre monté. Cook over low heat until the shrimp, and crab are fully cooked. Add the lemon juice and herbs, season to taste with salt and pepper and piment d'espelette. Set aside.

Cook the eggs over medium heat for 15-18 minutes, or until just set.

Beurre Monté

Bring 1 tablespoon of water to a boil in a saucepan. Bring the heat down to moderate and whisk in chunks of cold butter, 1 or 2 at a time. Once the butter has started to emulsify, more butter may be whisked in faster. Hold the beurre monté between 160-190° for poaching, being careful not to boil or it will break.

To Assemble and Serve

Reheat the green garlic sauce. Spoon some over each ramekin with eggs. Spoon seafood and mushroom sauté over the top. Serve with toast.

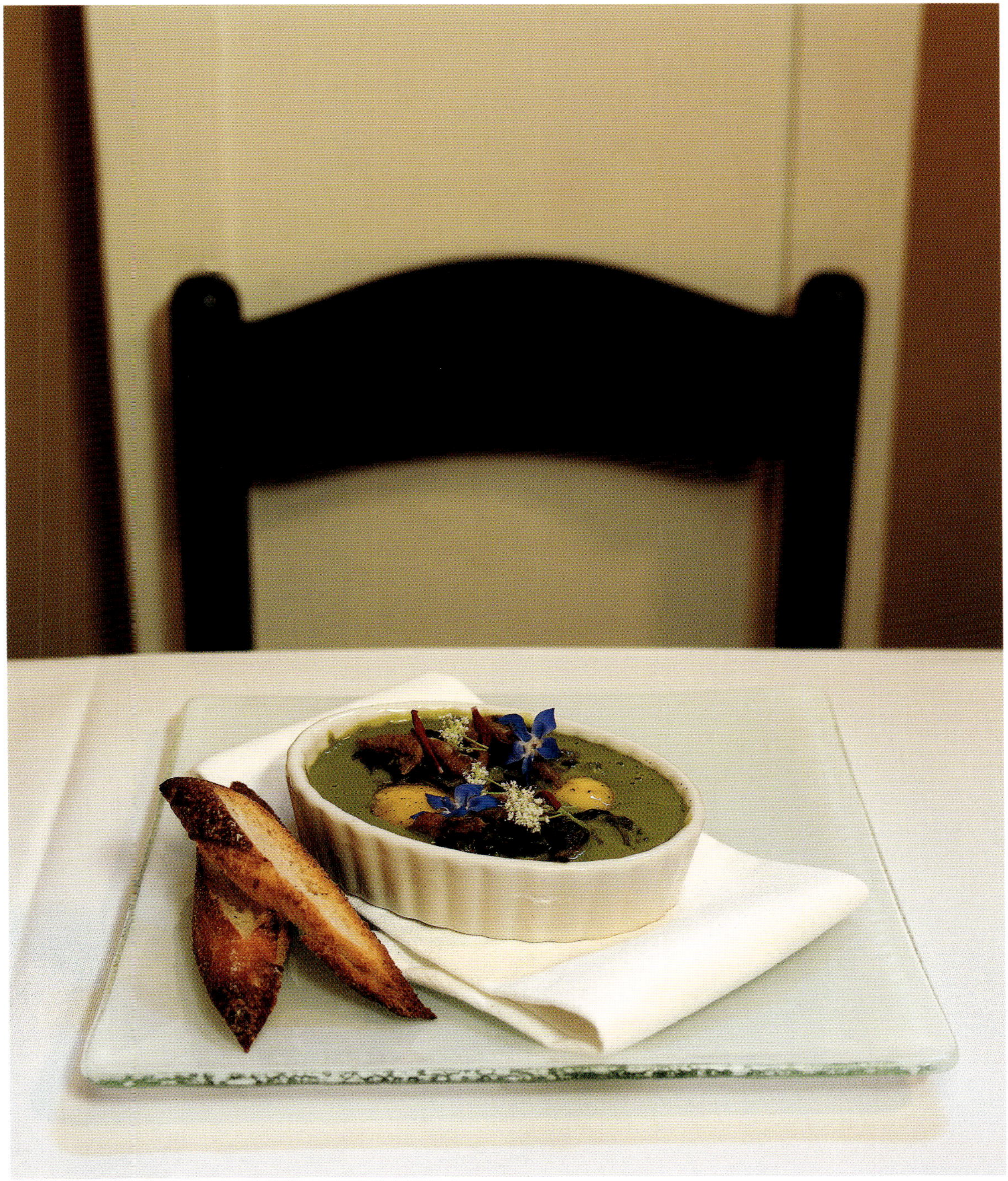

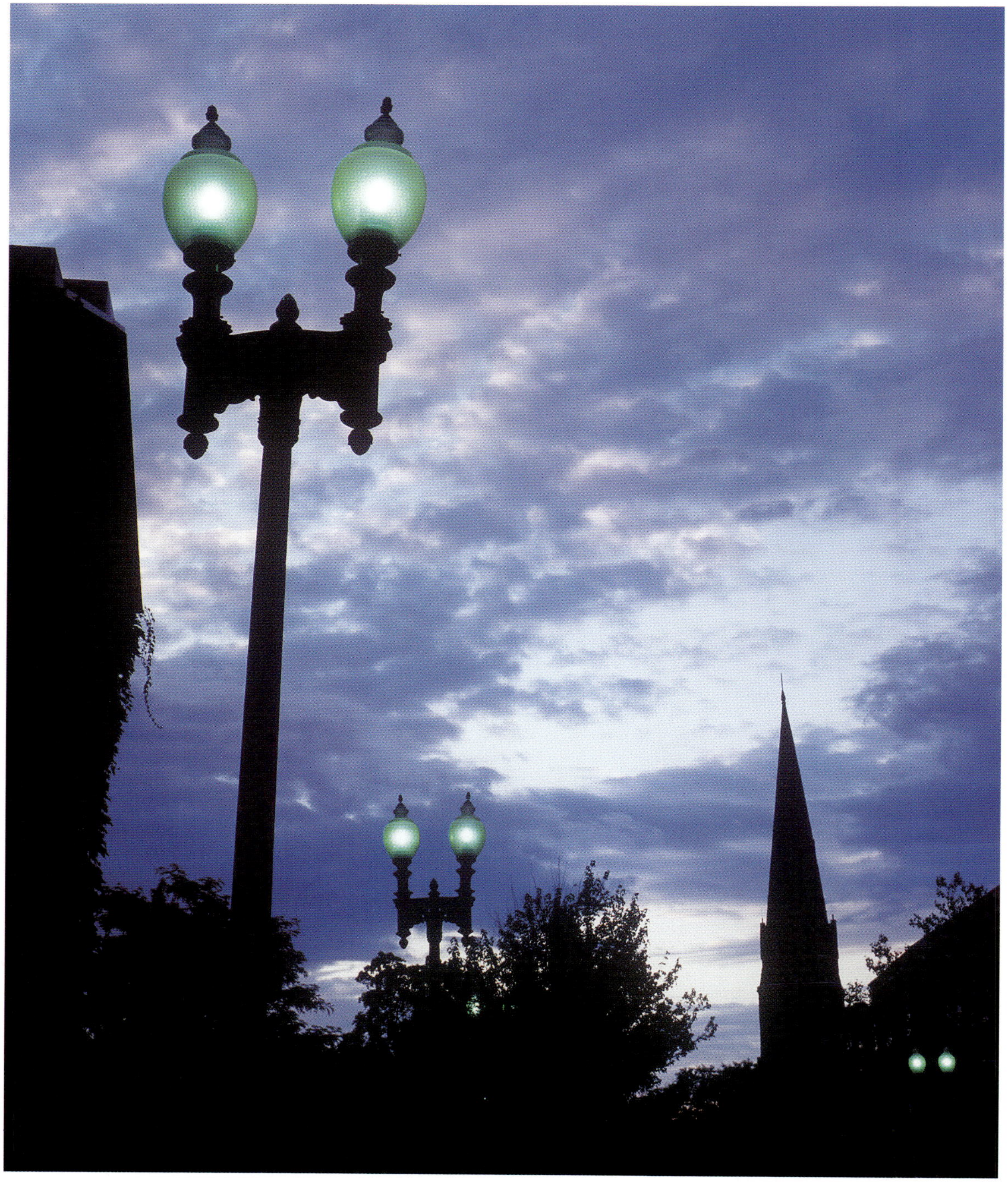

Casablanca

Sautéed Shrimp

1 head fennel, diced large
1 onion, diced large
2 poblano peppers, diced large
3 garlic cloves, crushed
¼ cup fresh dill, chopped
1 cup extra-virgin olive oil, plus more for bread
4 Roma tomatoes, blanched and skinned, diced large
¼ cup feta cheese
16 large shrimp, deveined
4 pieces thinly sliced crusty bread

Serves 4

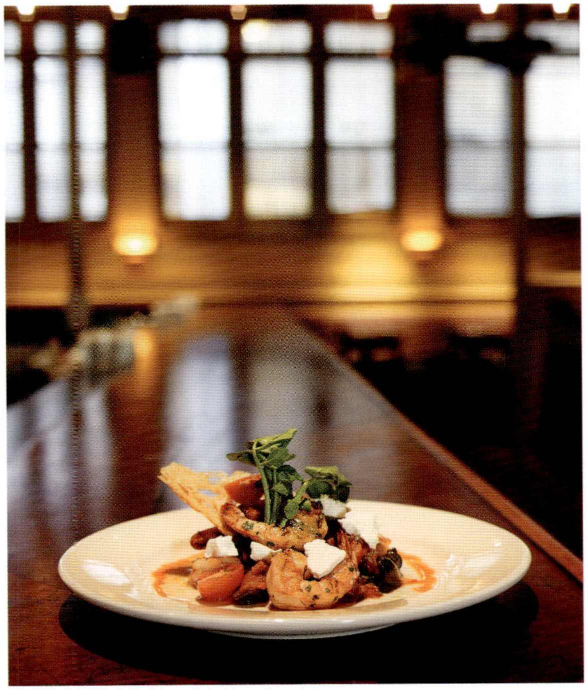

In a large pan, sauté the fennel and onions in the olive oil for 5 minutes. Add the peppers and garlic and cook for 5 more minutes. Add the tomatoes and dill and cook until the vegetables are tender. Season with salt and pepper.

Brush the bread with olive oil and toast in the oven on a sheet pan until crispy.

In a large pan, sear the shrimp. Once they've turned red, add the prepared vegetables and simmer until the shrimp are cooked through.

Place some of the vegetables and 4 shrimp on top of each crostini. Sprinkle with crumbled feta and serve.

Potato Gnocchi with Red Russian Kale and Fresh Ricotta

Gnocchi

5 large Idaho potatoes
1 egg
1 egg yolk
¼ cup grated Parmesan cheese
1 ½ cups all-purpose flour
salt to taste

Kale

1 pound Red Russian kale—or other variety available—stems removed and washed
extra-virgin olive oil
salt to taste

¼ pound good-quality fresh ricotta

Serves 4-6

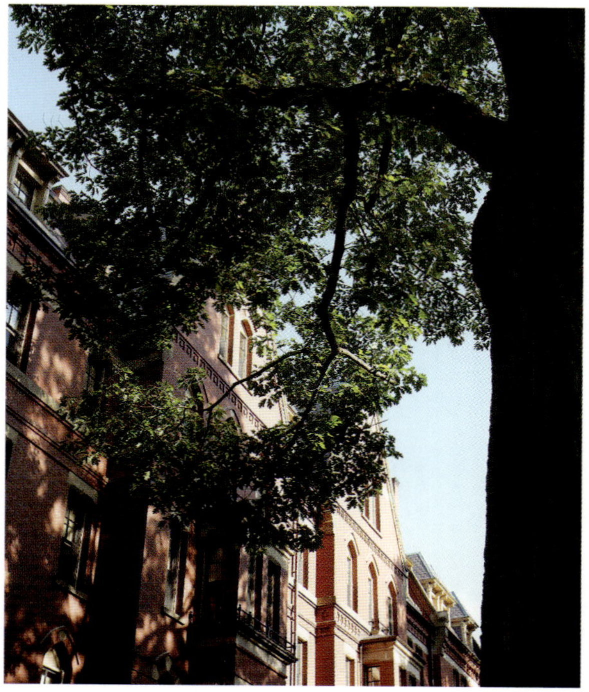

Place the potatoes in a large pot and cover with cold salted water. Simmer until fork-tender. While the potatoes are still hot, remove the skins with a paring knife, then pass the potatoes through the food mill into a large mixing bowl. Mix in the egg, egg yolk, cheese, salt, and flour until a uniform dough is achieved. The dough should be moist but not stick to your fingers; add more flour if necessary. Cut the dough into four equal pieces. On a floured work surface, roll the dough, by hand, into dowels about ¼-inch in diameter. Then cut the dowels into small pieces that resemble little pillows. Put the gnocchi in a large pot with simmering, salted water and cook until they float to the top. Remove from the water with a slotted spoon and place them in a bowl with a little oil so they won't stick to each other.

In a large sauté pan, heat olive oil until shimmering but not smoking. Carefully add the gnocchi and cook until golden brown on both sides. Remove them from the pan and place them on a paper towel to absorb any extra oil. Lightly sauté the kale in the same pan, adding salt to taste. Arrange the kale on a serving plate, then the gnocchi. Crumble ricotta over the dish and serve.

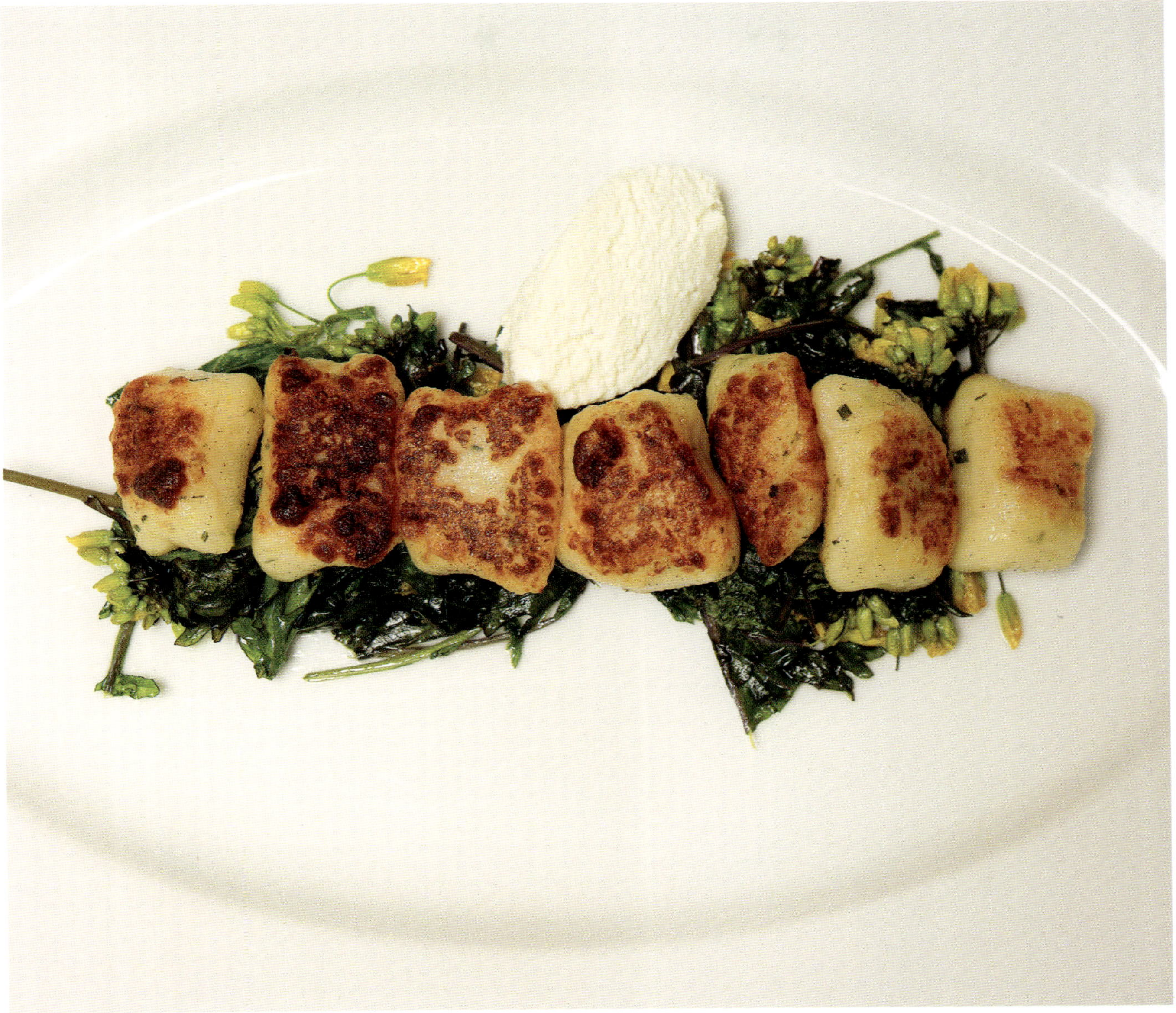

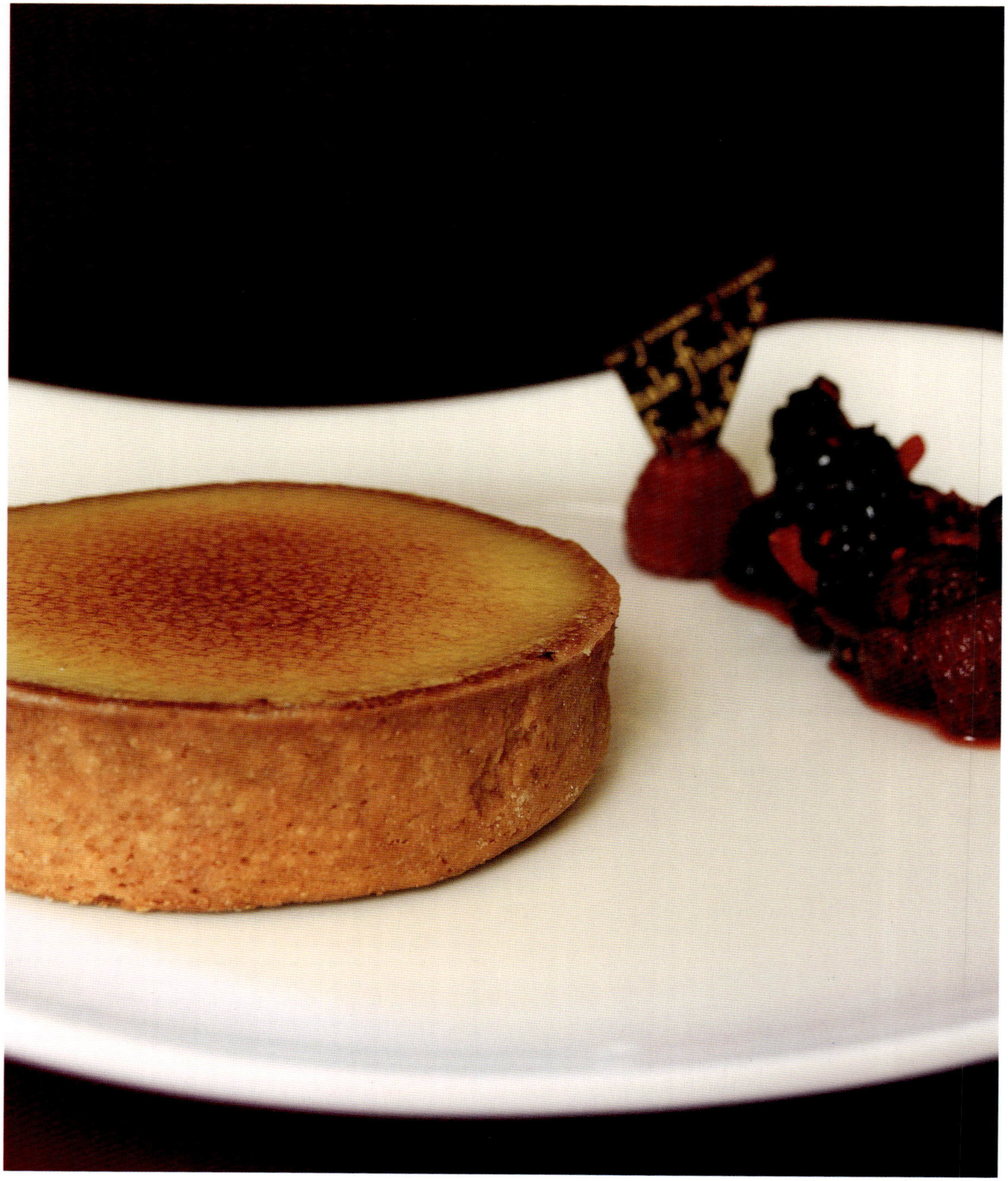

Lemon Tart with Mixed Berries

Lemon Curd

2½ sticks unsalted butter
5 eggs
5 medium lemons, juiced
1⅓ cups granulated sugar
Pinch kosher salt

Glazed Berries

⅓ cup blackberries
⅓ cup raspberries
⅓ cup strawberries, quartered
2 tablespoons superfine sugar

Lemon Curd

Break eggs into a metal mixing bowl and slightly mix. Add sugar and salt to the eggs and fully incorporate. Slowly incorporate lemon juice into the egg mixture until smooth. Bring a saucepan of water to a boil and reduce to a simmer. Place egg mixture over simmering water and stir occasionally, being sure to scrape down the sides when stirring. Heat the egg mixture until a candy thermometer reaches 180°. While heating, chop butter into small pieces and return to the refrigerator to keep cool. At 180°, remove the thickened egg mixture from the heat and allow to cool to 105°. Once the mixture reaches 105°, use a hand-held burr mixer to slowly incorporate the chopped butter. Cool the lemon curd till fully set.

Glazed Berries

Berries should be cut into comparable sizes. Toss them with sugar and let them marinate for at least 15 minutes. Adjust sugar according to the sweetness of the berries.

chapter two

SUMMER

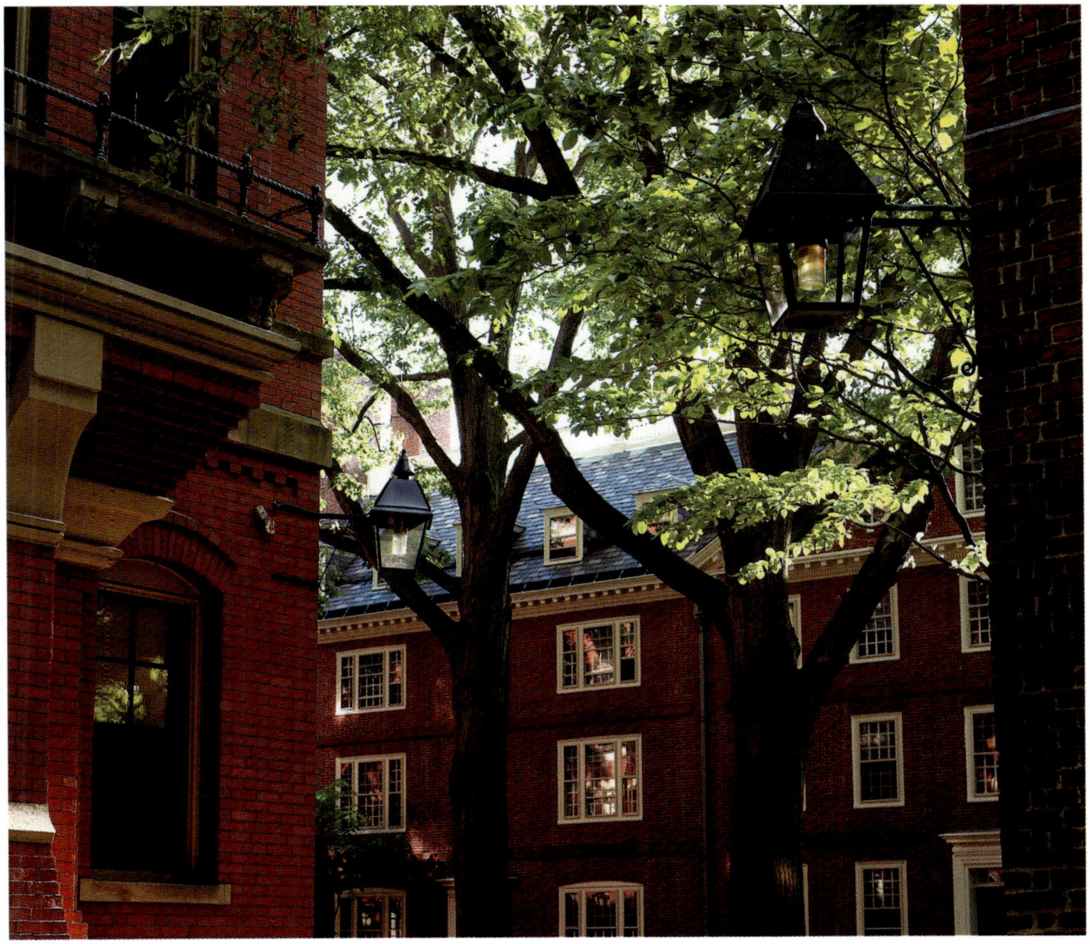

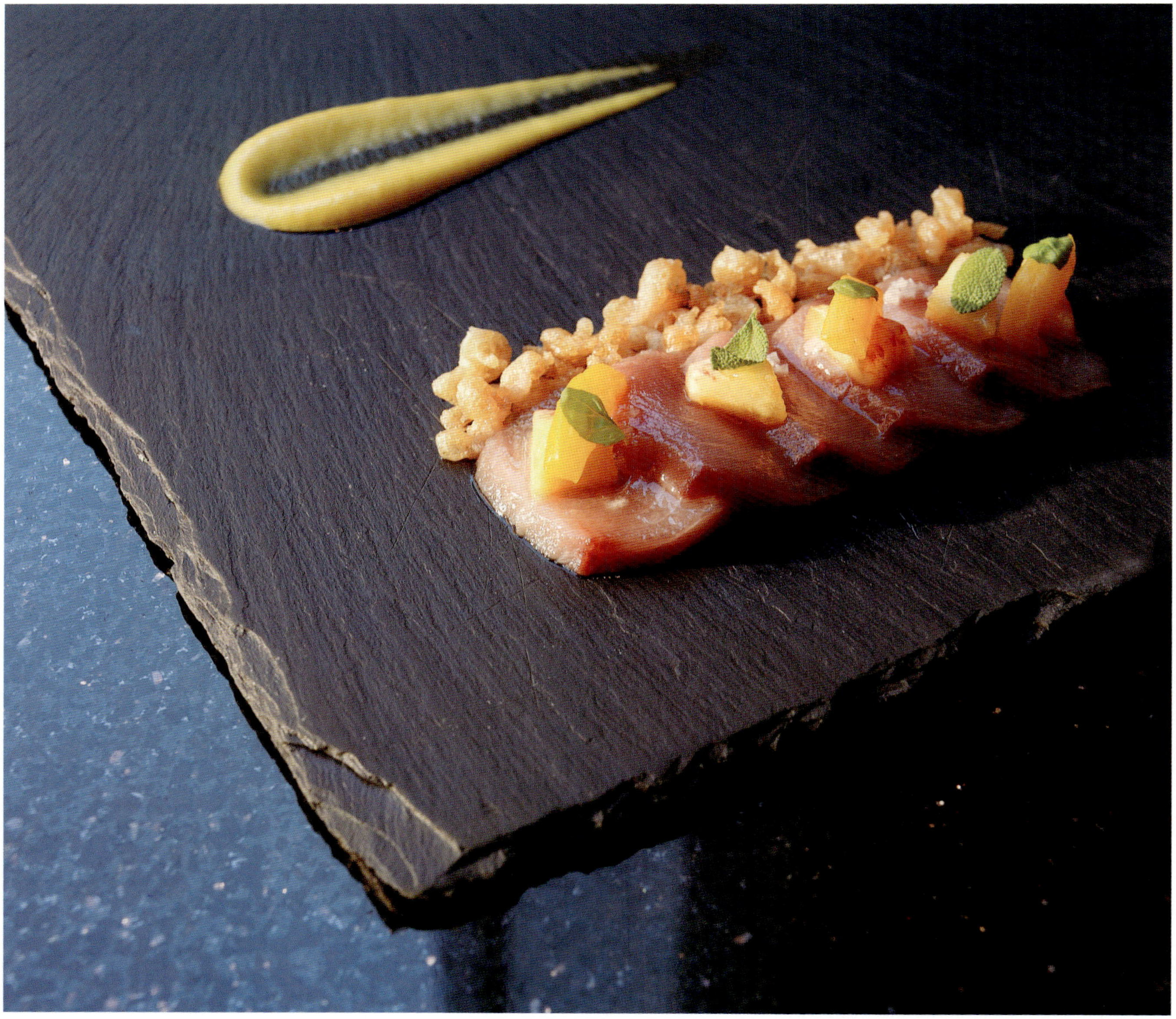

Hamachi, Sweet & Sour Peaches, Yellow Pepper Purée, and Mint

OM Restaurant

Hamachi

2 pounds hamachi
fleur de sel

Thai Syrup

1 quart water
1 cup granulated sugar
7 red Thai chils, sliced with seeds intact
2 slices ginger (1-inch coins), skin removed
zest of 1 lemon
1 cup mint

Sweet and Sour Peaches

2 tablespoons unsalted butter
2 quarts peaches, brunoised
1 quart champagne vinegar
1 quart light brown sugar
salt to taste

Yellow Peppers

5 yellow peppers, washed
½ cup champagne vinegar
1 cup water
2 tablespoons olive oil
kosher salt

Serves 6

Hamachi

Remove skin, any bones, and bloodline and cut fish into a rectangular block. Slice hamachi into ¼-inch slices (equaling 4-5 ounces per person). Place slices in Thai syrup and season with salt and pepper. Arrange peaches and peppers on the hamachi and sprinkle the fish with a few granules of fleur de sel. Spoon pepper purée onto plate. Garnish with mint leaves.

Thai Syrup

In a nonreactive saucepot, mix all ingredients together except the mint. Bring to a boil and reduce to a simmer. Reduce by half, or until syrupy. Remove from the heat and add mint. Let the mint steep 3 minutes. Strain and cool.

Sweet and Sour Peaches

Melt butter on low heat in a nonreactive sauté pan. Turn heat to medium-high and add peaches and toss with butter. Add all other ingredients and bring to a simmer. Cook until liquid has evaporated by ¾ or peaches are soft but still hold their shape. Cool a on sheet pan in the refrigerator. Store in their liquid.

Yellow Peppers

Coat the peppers with olive oil and season with kosher salt. Place in a shallow roasting pan. Add water and vinegar to the pan. Cover with foil, shiny side up. Place in oven at 350° and cook until peppers are soft. Reserve half of the peppers for the pepper purée. Cut the other half into 1-x-½-inch strips. Reserve in strained cooking liquid until ready to use. For the pepper purée, place the reserved peppers in a blender. Purée. Check for salt.

Grilled Clams on the Half Shell with Garlic Crostini

1-2 cups kosher salt, as needed
24 scrubbed fresh littleneck clams (3½-4 pounds)
freshly ground white pepper (substitute freshly ground black pepper if white pepper is only available pre-ground)
1 cup extra-virgin olive oil
1 loaf rustic bread, cut into 1½-inch slices
6 garlic cloves, peeled
12 diagonally cut ½-inch slices andouille sausage
4 lemon wedges

Makes 24 hors d'oeuvres

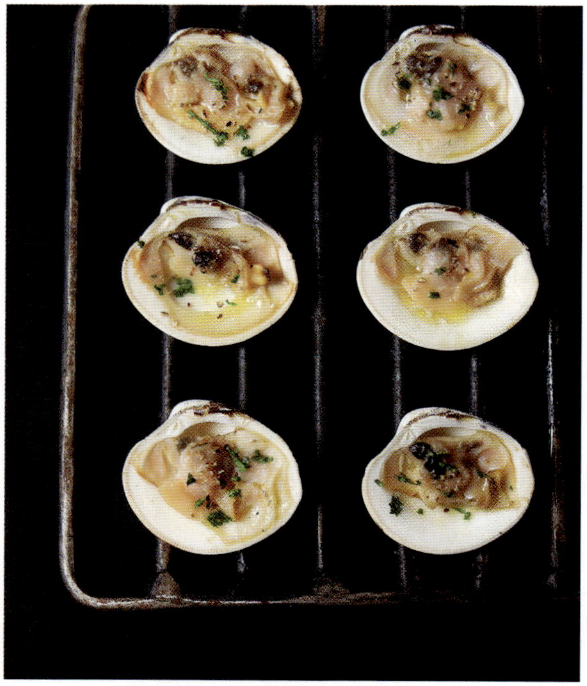

Prepare a grill with both hot and medium sections. A grill is hot when you can hold your hand near the cooking surface for no more than a count of 2 before having to pull it away. For the medium section of the grill you should be able to hold your hand near the cooking surface for at least a count of 4 before having to pull it away.

Cover a large platter with a ½-inch layer of kosher salt. Open the clams and set each clam in its half shell on the salted platter. The salt prevents the clams from tipping. The clams cook—and stay moist—in their own juice, or "liquor." Preserve as much of this flavorful liquid as possible while opening the clams. Sprinkle the clams with pepper and drizzle each clam with about ½ teaspoon olive oil—don't measure, just drizzle lightly.

To make the crostini, brush the bread slices with olive oil. Place the slices on the medium part of the grill. Grill until toasted, 1 or 2 minutes on each side—watch them carefully so they don't burn. Rub the grilled slices with raw garlic and sprinkle with salt. Cut the crostini crosswise so you have 24 pieces and stack on a platter.

Grill the sausages on each side until seared and warmed through. Transfer to the platter with the crostini.

Using tongs, place the clams, in their shells, on the hot grill. Watch for the liquor and olive oil to boil. Allow the clams to boil until they're just cooked—depending on the temperature of the grill, this may take only 1 minute. Err on the side of under-doneness. Transfer the clams from the grill back to the platter. If they're a shade underdone—a matter of taste—you can always put them back on the grill for a few seconds. Serve the clams, sausage, and crostini immediately. Offer lemon wedges on the side.

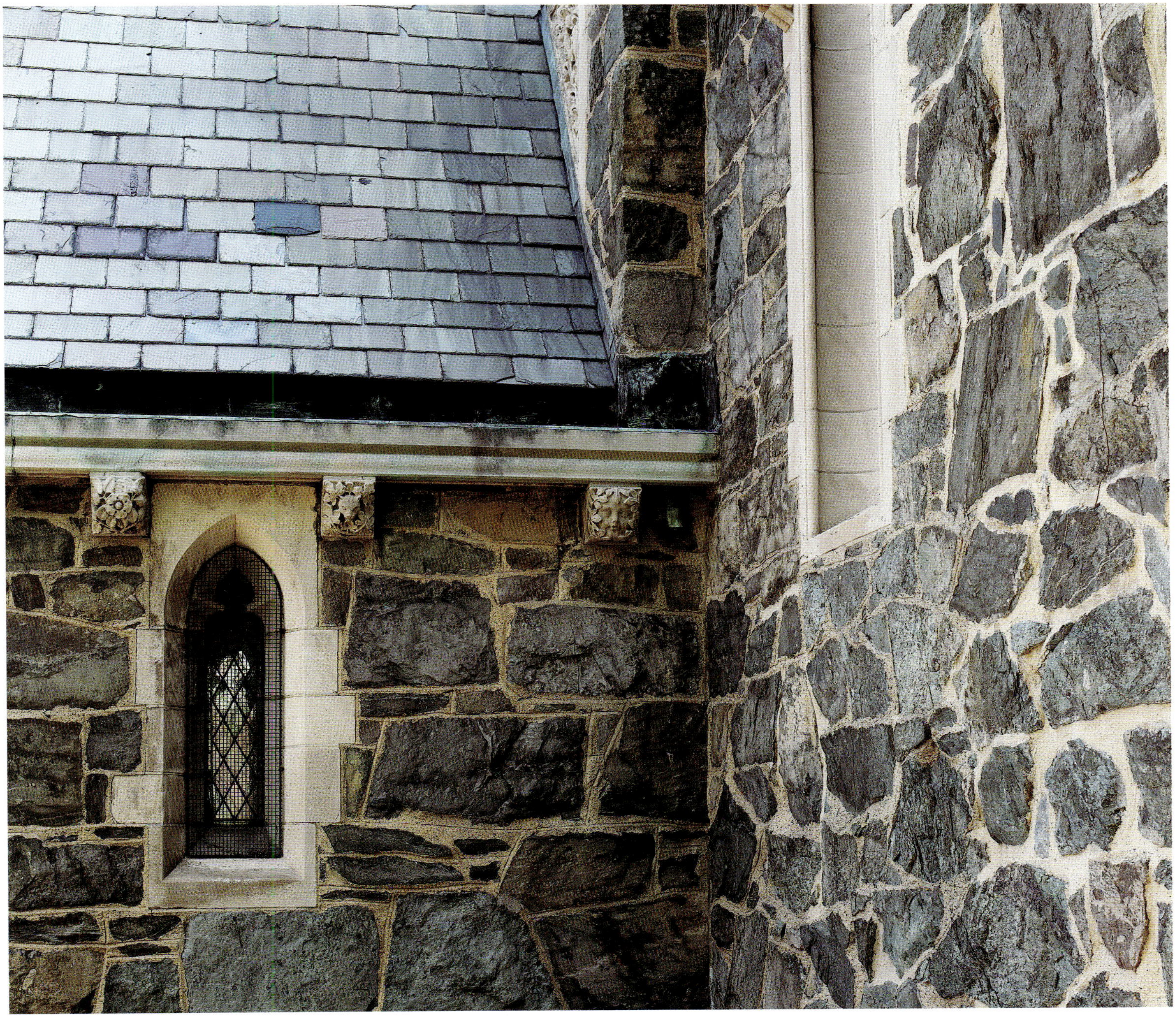

RIALTO

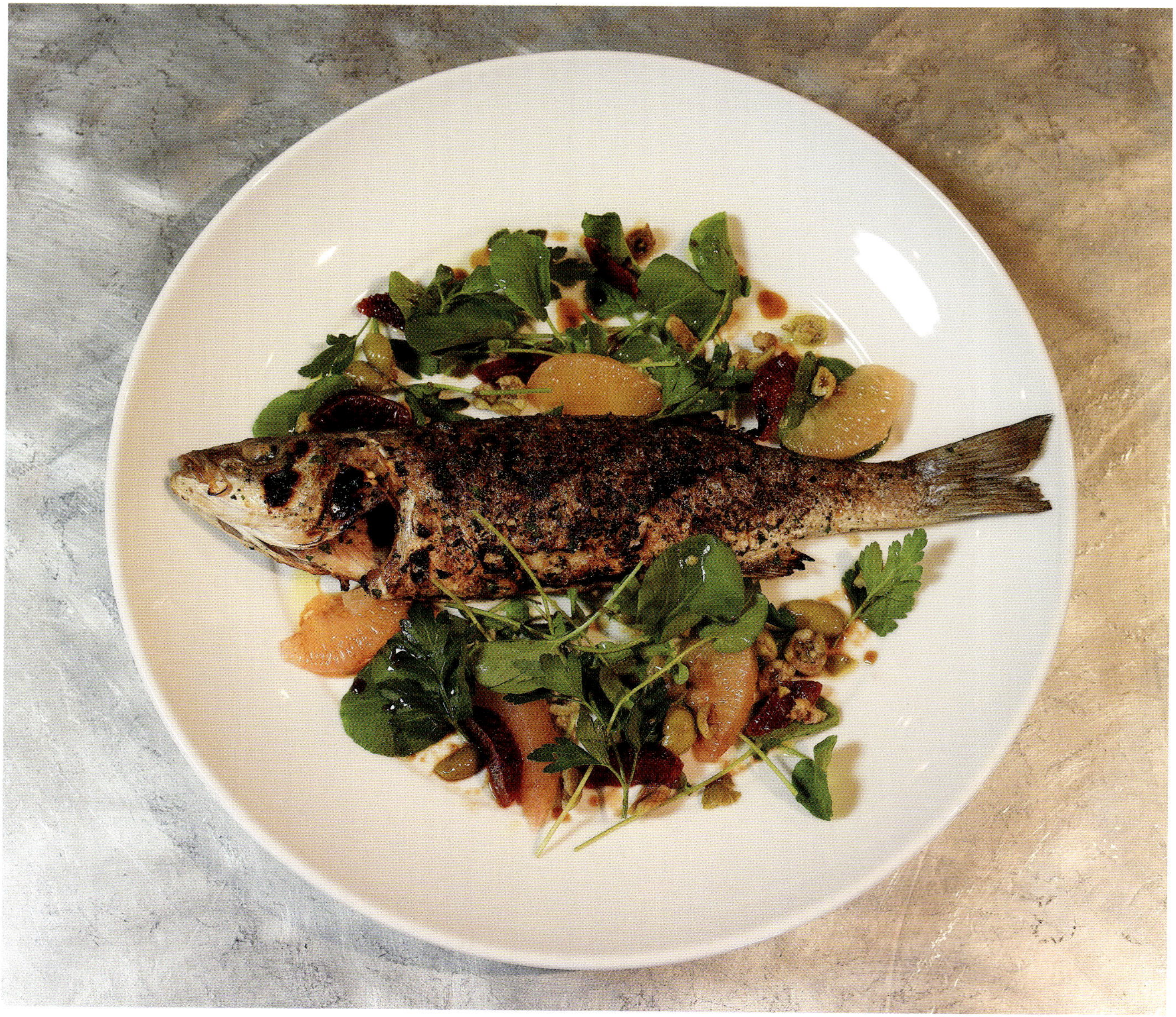

Branzino with Green Olives

Served with Grapefruit Salad and Pomegranate Vinaigrette

Branzino

4 branzino or Mediterranean sea bass

Salad

1 cup pitted green Picholine olives or Lucques
2 pink grapefruit, peeled and sectioned
2 bunches watercress, washed and stemmed
1 bunch Italian parsley, washed and stemmed
3 sprigs mint, washed and stemmed
sea salt and white pepper

Pomegranate Vinaigrette

2 tablespoons pomegranate syrup or molasses
½ cup extra-virgin olive oil
¼ cup lemon juice
sea salt

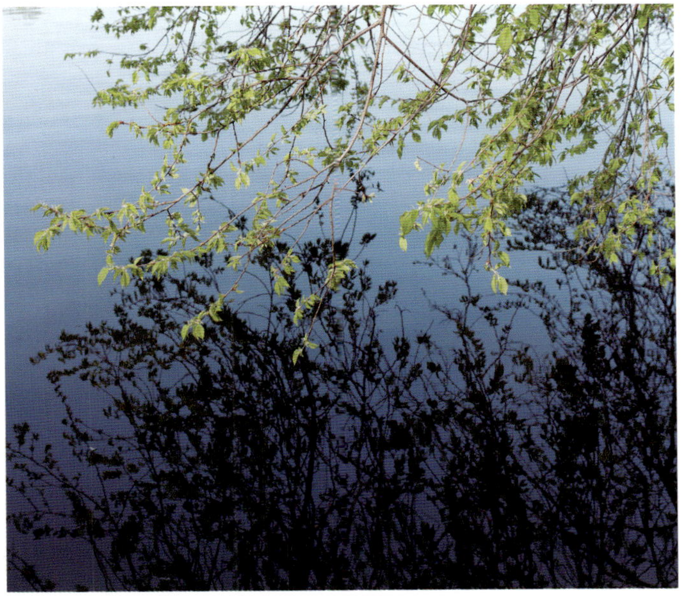

When you buy the branzino, ask the fish monger to "dress" it. This means that he or she will scale and gut the fish. You can also ask to have the gills and fins removed, or you can do it yourself; it is necessary that the gills and fins be removed, however, to serve the dish properly.

Season the cavity and the exterior of the fish with sea salt and white pepper. Rub a small amount of extra-virgin olive oil on the skin, being careful not to use too much—½ teaspoon per fish will suffice.

To prepare the vinaigrette, combine the syrup, lemon juice, and sea salt and slowly whisk as you pour the extra-virgin olive oil in a steady stream. Set aside.

Place the fish on a well-cleaned and well-oiled spot on the grill over medium-high heat. The goal is to flip the fish just once, so be patient—if the fish is sticking to the grill, it's not ready to be flipped; wait until it lifts from the grill easily. It will take approximately 8 minutes. Follow the same guidelines with respect to the other side. Remove from the grill and distribute to plates.

To prepare the salad, simply toss the pitted olives, grapefruit sections, watercress, parsley, and mint together in a bowl. Add vinaigrette to taste—roughly half of the vinaigrette. Save the rest for the fish and the plate.

Mound the grapefruit-olive salad on top of the fish and drizzle the remaining vinaigrette on top. This dish tastes especially good with roasted potatoes.

Summer Raspberry Tartlet

Shortbread Shell

¾ cup butter
½ cup sugar
1½ cups all-purpose flour
1 teaspoon salt
1 teaspoon vanilla
white chocolate

Raspberry Filling

½ cup sugar
1 teaspoon lemon zest
3 pints local raspberries
1 tablespoon honey

Sweet Raspberry Fool

2 tablespoons sugar
½ cup fresh raspberries
1 pint heavy cream
¼ cup crème fraîche
1 dash cinnamon

Shortbread Shell

Cream butter and sugar, then add vanilla, flour, and salt. Mix until just combined. Roll to ¼-inch thick and chill for one hour, then cut and press into greased tart shell. Line tart shell with paper and fill with any kind of beans—this keeps the sides of the shell from sinking. Bake at 350° for 8-10 minutes, then remove the beans and bake for an additional 5 minutes. When cool, remove shell from pan and line with melted white chocolate.

Raspberry Filling

Combine zest and sugar and rub between your hands to release oils. Toss the raspberries with the sugar and honey and fill the tart shell.

Raspberry Fool

Combine sugar and raspberries and mash with a fork. Whip the cream and add the raspberries, crème fraîche, and cinnamon. This will loosen the cream, so rewhip until firm. Chill and serve very cold.

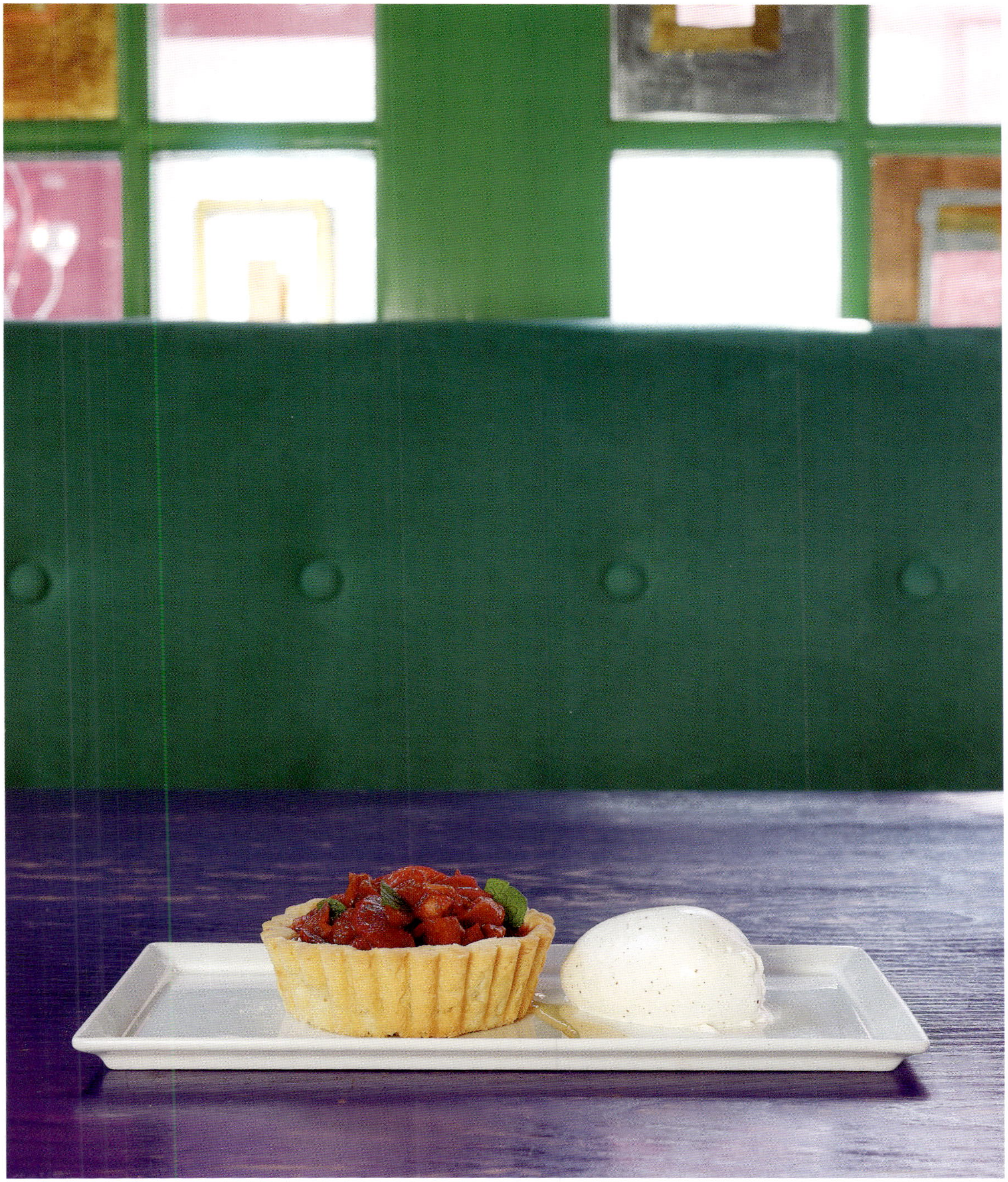

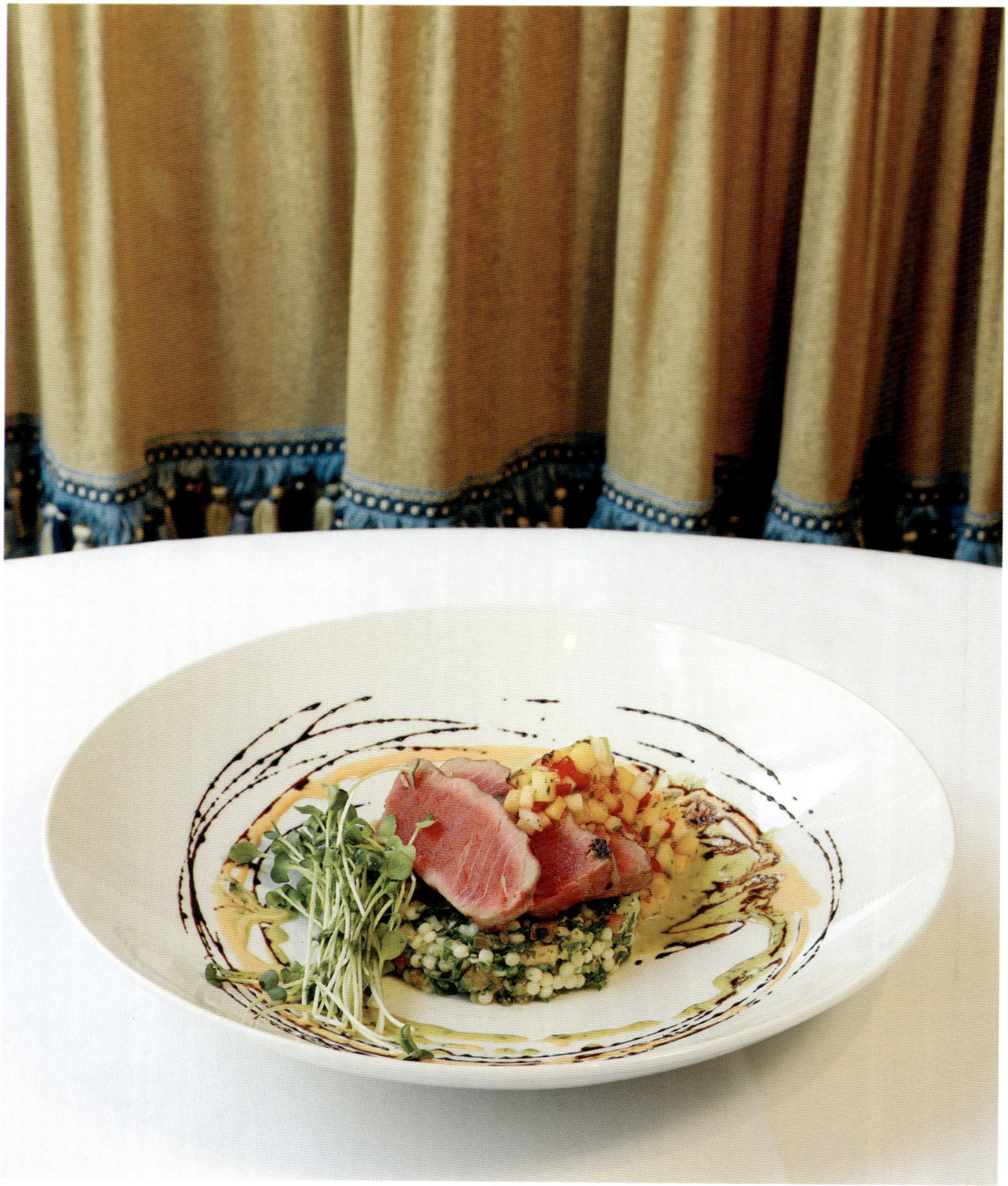

Grilled Tuna with Couscous Tabbouleh

6 ounces center cut tuna steak per person
olive oil, sea salt, and pepper

Couscous Tabbouleh

1 box couscous, small grain
3 plum tomatoes, chopped
2 bunches flat parsley, roughly chopped
1 red onion, chopped
½ bunch scallions, chopped
1 lemon, juiced
½ cup olive oil
6 sprigs lemon verbena for garnish, optional

Dressing

1 cup olive oil
2 lemons, juiced
1 tablespoon Dijon mustard
4 cloves garlic, chopped
½ bunch mint, chopped
1 bunch tarragon, leaves only
2 roasted red peppers, seeded and skinned

Tropical Fruit Chutney

1 pineapple, peeled, cored, and diced
2 mangoes, diced
1 red onion, diced
2 tomatoes, diced
½ bunch mint, chopped
½ bunch parsley, chopped
2 lemons, juiced
2 tablespoons honey
4 cloves of garlic, chopped
½-1 habanero pepper, chopped

Serves 6

Served with tropical fruit chutney and mint-tarragon dressing

Grilled Tuna

Brush tuna with olive oil and season with sea salt and pepper. Grill for 2 minutes on each side for medium-rare.

Couscous Tabbouleh

Cook couscous as directed on box. Cool completely. Add the tomatoes, parsley, red onion, scallions, lemon, and olive oil and mix well. Season with salt and pepper to taste.

Tropical Fruit Chutney

Please note: habanero peppers are extremely hot, so wear gloves and use sparingly. Mix all ingredients together and macerate for 24 hours.

To Serve

Arrange tuna steak and 2 tablespoons of fruit chutney on a bed of tabbouleh, drizzle the plate with dressing, and add lemon verbena for garnish.

Duck Tamale with Spinach Salad and Chipotle Vinaigrette

6 cups Masa Harina flour
3-4 cups chicken stock
4 ounces butter
2 tablespoons salt
2 cups duck confit, shredded
3 ounces of duck fat or canola oil
1 cup onions, minced
½ cup red pepper, minced
3 tablespoons garlic, minced
1 tablespoon black pepper
¼ cup scallions, minced
4 tablespoons cilantro, minced
2-3 ounces lime juice

Chipotle Vinaigrette

2 chipolte chilis
2 ounces adobo sauce
2 teaspoons garlic, minced
3 ounces red wine vinegar
6 ounces olive oil

Spinach Salad

4 bunches washed spinach
2 cups radicchio, julienne
1½ cups bacon cracklings, ¼-inch diced
¼ cup bacon fat
6 teaspoons grain mustard
½ cup red wine vinegar
black pepper

Bring the chicken stock and butter to a boil in a small saucepot. Remove from heat and set aside.

Place the masa in a mixer with a paddle attachment or a food processor. On a medium speed, begin adding the butter, chicken stock, and salt to the masa. Don't worry about over-mixing the dough; it will not become tough. The dough should have a playdough consistency. Place dough in a bowl and cover tightly with plastic wrap. Store at room temperature until you are ready to use it. Refrigerate if you won't be using it for more than 3 hours.

Heat a large sauté pan over medium-high heat. Add duck fat or canola oil to the pan. Add the onion, red pepper, jalapeño, and garlic and cook until the onions are translucent.

Add the duck confit and mix together well, while cooking over a moderate heat. Remove from the heat and season with black pepper. Add the cilantro, scallions, and lime juice. Stir and taste. Cool the filling before assembling the tamales. Assemble the tamales—see below—using cornhusks as the wrapper or buttered aluminum foil. Steam the tamales over a double boiler for at least 20 minutes.

Tamale Technique

Lay the cornhusk or foil wrapper on a flat surface. Using your hands or a rubber spatula, spread the masa dough in ¼-inch layer to form a 3-x-5-inch rectangle. Trim the edges and square off with a knife. Spread 4 ounces or ¼ cup of the duck filling down the center of the dough, covering ⅓ of the surface area.

Bring the 2 wide ends together to enclose the filling, overlapping the corn husk. Make sure the dough fully encloses the filling. Tie the ends with string or strands of the corn husk.

Chipotle Vinaigrette

Place all of the ingredients in a blender and purée. Strain through a fine sieve and place in a squeeze bottle.

Spinach Salad

Place the washed and dried spinach in a large bowl along with the radicchio. Heat the bacon and its fat in a small pan until the bacon is hot. Stir in the mustard, red wine vinegar, and black pepper. Spoon the dressing over the salad and toss well.

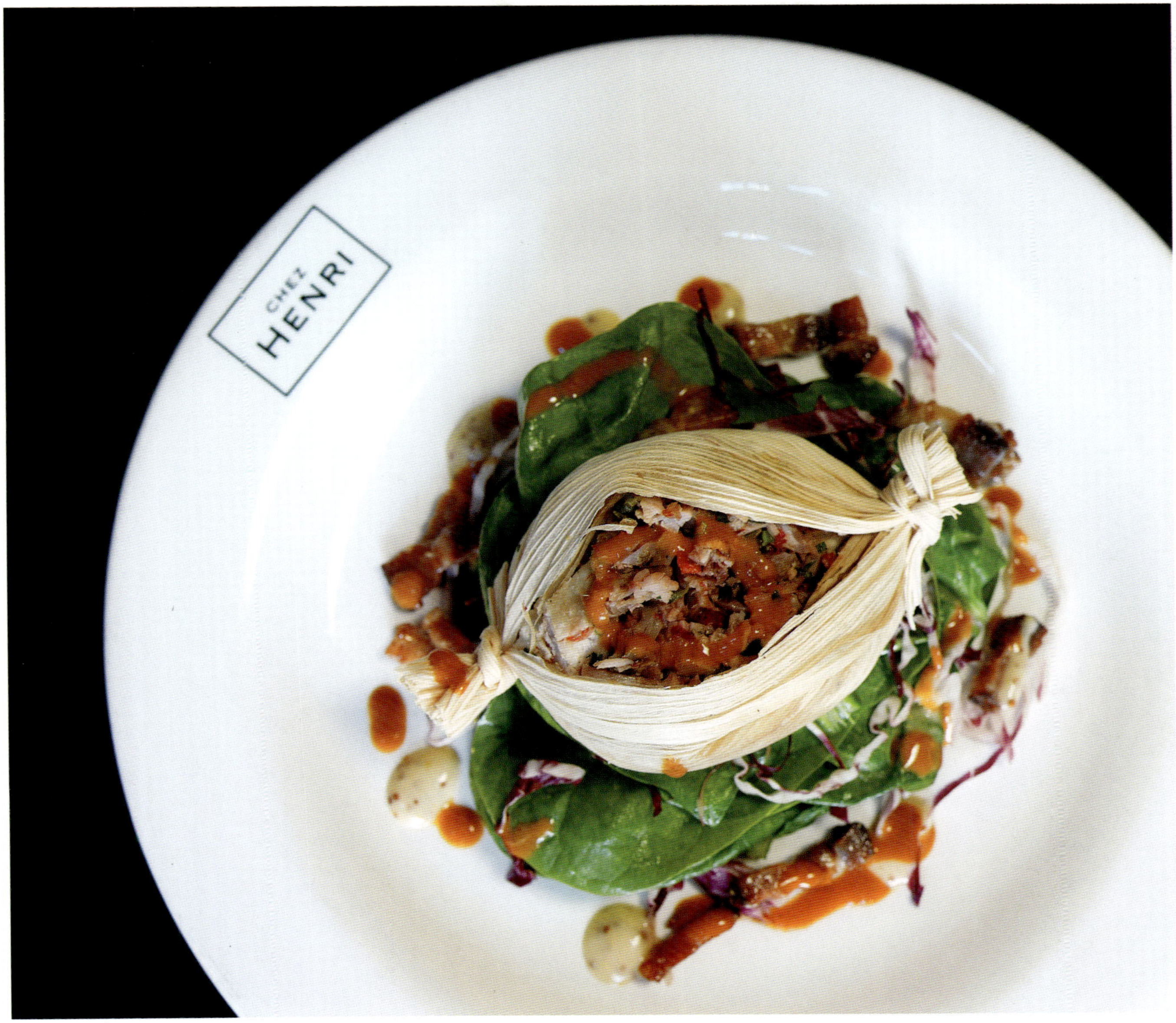
CHEZ
HENRI

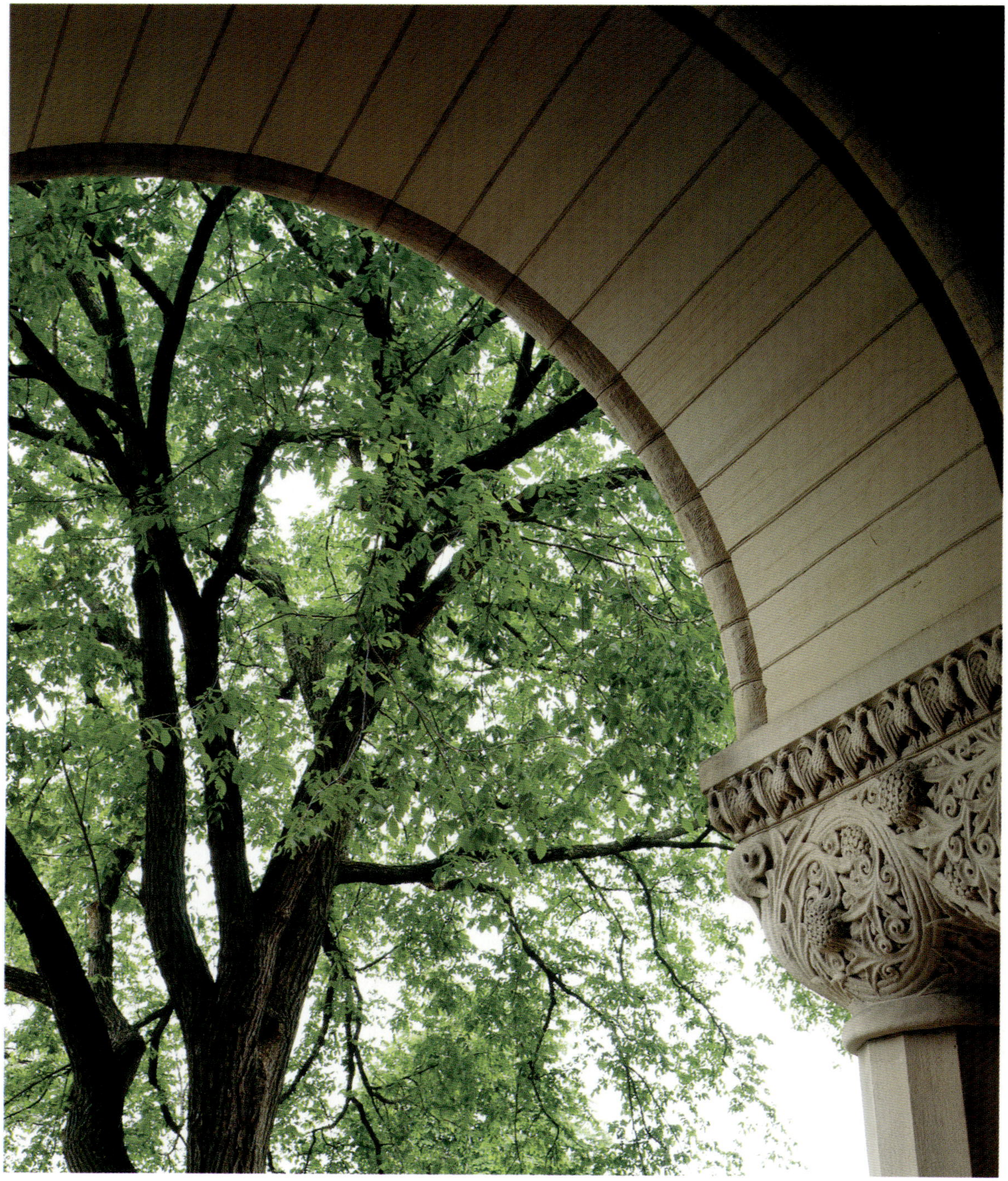

Tea-Smoked Bluefish Cakes with Togarashi Aioli

Tea-Smoked Bluefish

1 cup wood chips (Hickory, apple, or cherry)
1 cup black tea leaves
½ cup uncooked jasmine rice
2 pounds super-fresh bluefish filet (skin on, scaled)
¼ cup canola oil
kosher salt and freshly ground black pepper

Bluefish Cakes

2 ounces unsalted butter
½ cup finely diced onion
½ cup finely diced celery
½ cup finely diced red bell pepper
2 cups flaked, tea smoked blue fish
½ cup small toasted bread cubes
½ cup togarashi aioli plus ½ cup additional for garnish (Recipe follows)
1 egg
2 thinly sliced scallions, green part only
1 tablespoon chopped cilantro
juice of ¼ lemon
salt and freshly ground black pepper
canola oil for cooking
½ cup baby cilantro or baby greens for garnish

Togarashi Aioli

⅛ cup shichimi togarashi (Japanese 7-spice blend)
1 tablespoon Dijon mustard
4 egg yolks
1 teaspoon minced garlic
pinch sugar
1 teaspoon fresh lemon juice
1 cup canola oil
kosher salt

Serves 4-6

Tea Smoked Bluefish

Let the wood chips soak for at least one hour in water. Preheat a charcoal or gas grill to low heat. Place the wood chips, tea leaves, and rice onto a double-thick piece of aluminum foil and set directly on the coals. If using a gas grill place the foil on a hot spot in the grill. Rub the top side of the fish with canola oil and season well with salt and pepper. Once the wood chips are smoking, lay the fish filet skin-side down on a piece of foil. Place the fish in a cool area and cover the grill with a lid. Let the filet smoke approximately 30 minutes. The fish should be gently cooked through and not dry.

Let the fish cool to room temperature. Peel the skin off the back of the fillet and gently scrap out the dark areas with a knife. Carefully scrape out the ridge of thin bones near the thickest part of the filet. Flake the remaining fish into small pieces. Use immediately or store in the refrigerator for up to 4 days.

Bluefish Cakes

Melt the butter over medium heat in a small sauté pan. Add the onion, celery, and red bell pepper and cook for 5 minutes. Let cool completely. In a bowl, mix together all the ingredients except the last 3, including the cooked vegetables. Season the mix with salt and freshly ground black pepper. Shape into 3 or 4 ounce cakes and refrigerate for ½ hour. Preheat a nonstick pan over medium heat and coat the pan with a very small amount of canola oil. Cook the cakes for about 3 minutes on each side until golden-brown. Serve hot with a dollop of the reserved aioli and the baby cilantro or greens on top.

To Garashi Aioli

Add the togarashi, Dijon, egg yolk, garlic, sugar, and lemon juice to the bowl of a small food processor. Purée until smooth, making sure to scrape the sides with a rubber spatula. With the machine running, slowly drizzle in the canola oil, forming an emulsion. If the aioli gets too thick, a few drops of cold water can be added.

Chilled Rhubarb Soup

8-10 stalks rhubarb, rinsed well
4-5 sprigs of tarragon
1 small knob ginger, sliced and smashed
1 vanilla bean, split and scraped
approximately ½ cup vanilla sugar
1 tablespoon hibiscus tea, in a sachet
1-2 ounces white wine
pinch salt

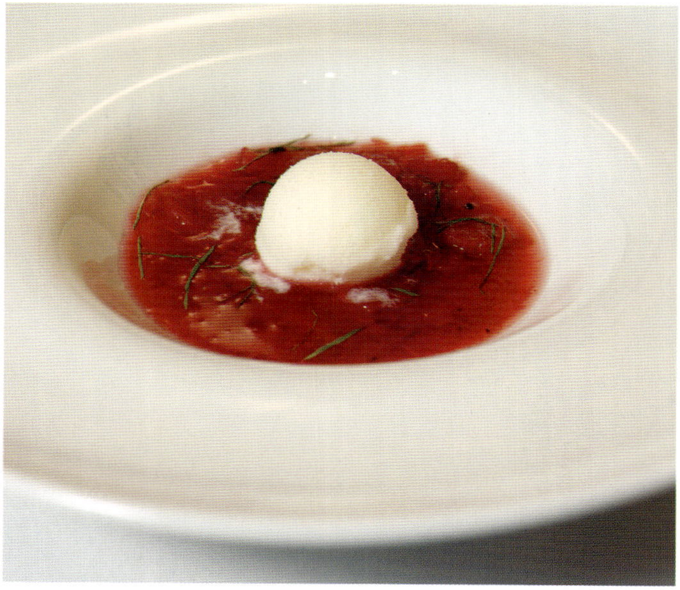

Slice rhubarb into ⅛-inch discs. Combine everything but the hibiscus tea in a large pot. Cover with water and bring to a boil. Add tea and let steep for 3 minutes. Remove sachet. Put into a large bowl, which you put in a larger bowl filled with ice cubes or water. Top with fresh tarragon, mint, or fennel. As an added bonus, you could top the soup with a lovely vanilla or crème fraîche ice cream or a berry sorbet.

Vanilla Sugar

To make vanilla sugar, save used vanilla pods and leave above the stove until dry—a few hours. Then simply place in a mason jar and cover with sugar. Use whenever sugar is called for in recipes.

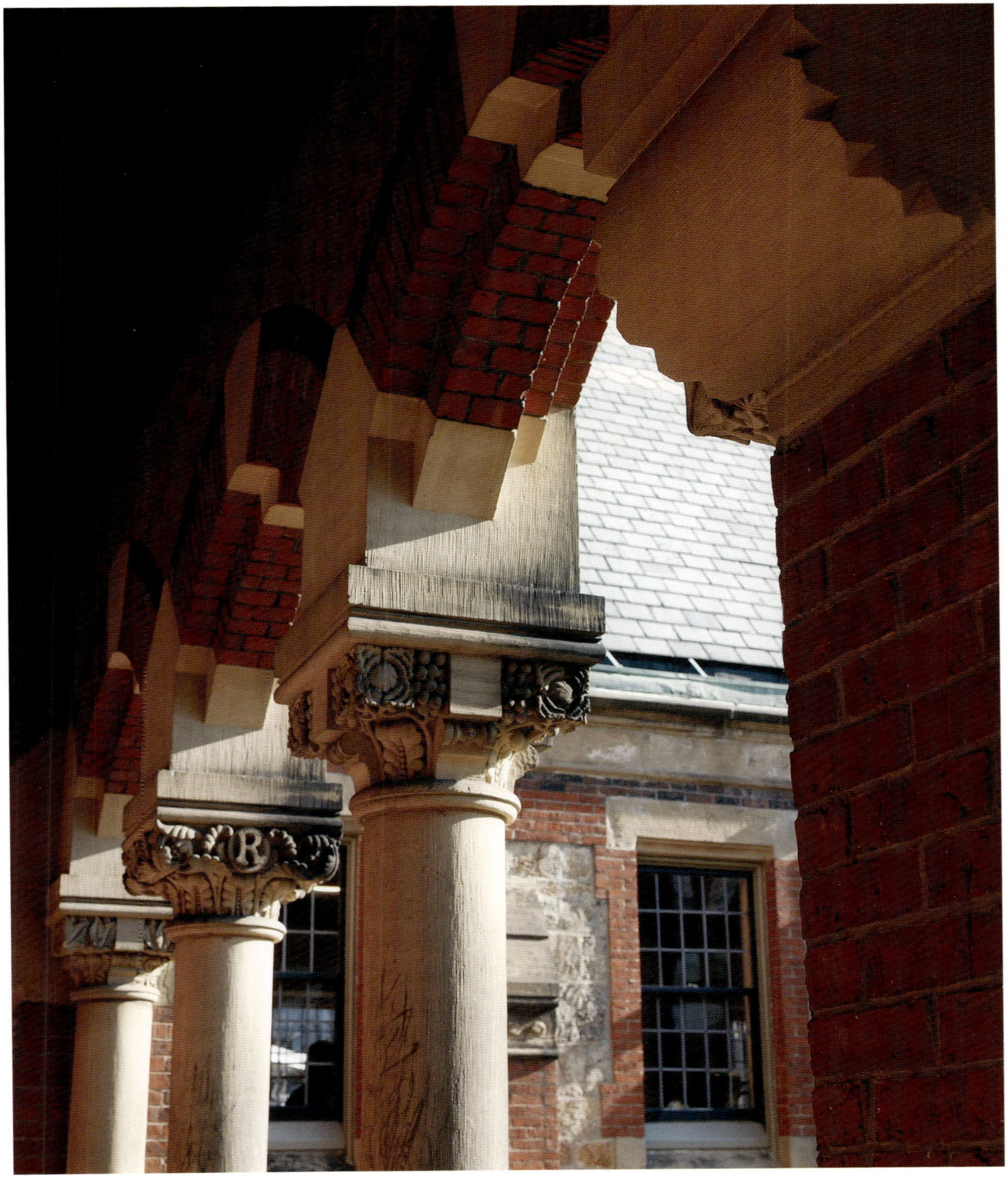

Craigie Street Bistrot

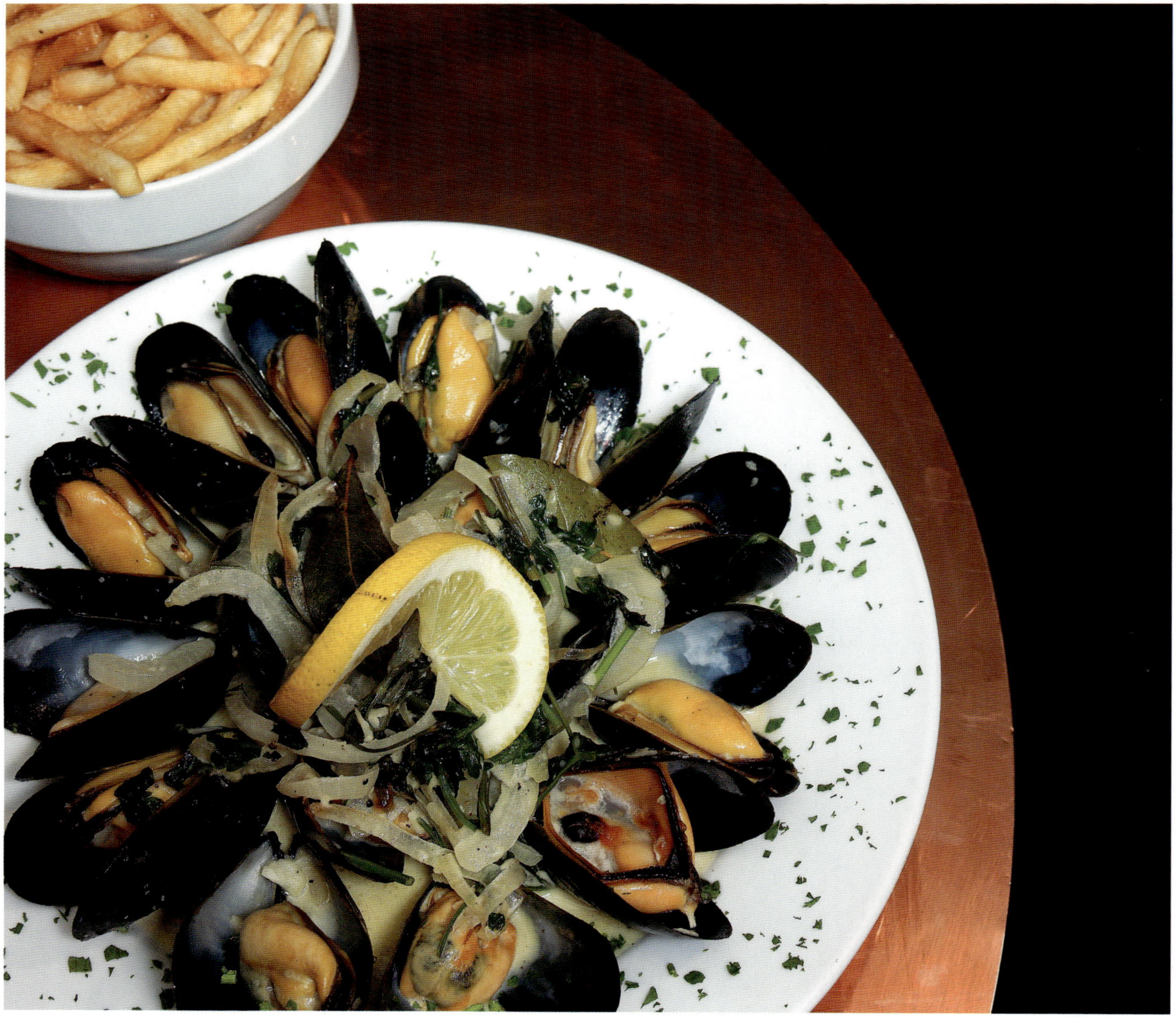

Moules Frites

4 pounds P.E.I. mussels
¼ cup olive oil
1 onion, chopped
1 tablespoon chopped garlic
2 bay leaves
4 sprigs parsley
2 slices of lemon per serving
1 pinch salt and pepper
2 cups chicken stock
½ cup heavy cream
1 pound French fries

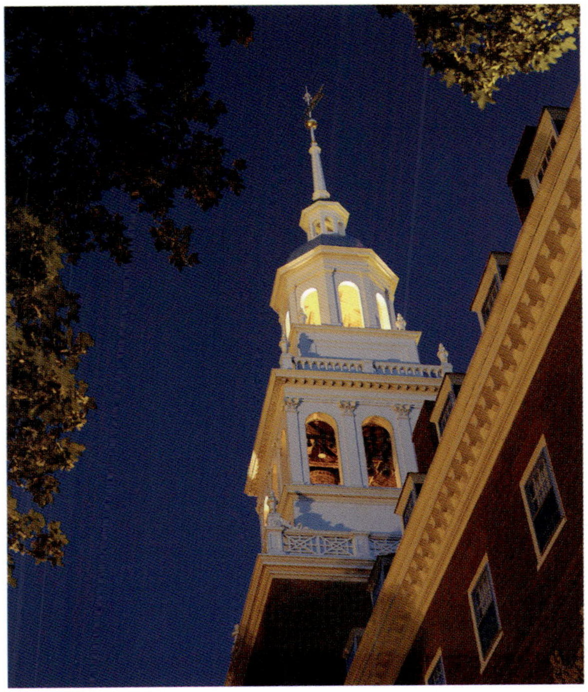

Rinse the mussels quickly under cold water. P.E.I. mussels are usually sold clean and ready for cooking.

In a pot over medium heat, sauté the onions, garlic, parsley, lemon, and bay leaves in the olive oil for 2 minutes. Add the mussels, salt, and pepper and keep stirring. Deglaze the pan with white wine and cook for 1 to 2 minutes. Add the chicken stock and heavy cream. Stir to mix the heavy cream with the rest of the liquid and cover to steam the mussels. Cook for another 3 to 4 minutes. (Cooking time depends on the size of the mussels, so be sure to stir the mussels constantly and don't overcook them; their texture becomes rubbery if they're cooked too long.)

Before serving, season again with salt and pepper to taste. Serve French fries on the side. This dish is traditionally served in French bistros and brasseries (the dish is Belgian in origin) and accompanied with beer.

White Gazpacho

½ DAY-OLD BAGUETTE
3 CUPS WHOLE BLANCHED ALMONDS
4 CUPS GREEN GRAPES
5 CLOVES GARLIC
1½ LITERS MINERAL WATER
8 TABLESPOONS SHERRY VINEGAR
OLIVE OIL
SEA SALT AND WHITE PEPPER TO TASTE
RADISHES, GRAPES, AND TOASTED ALMONDS FOR GARNISH

SERVES 6-8

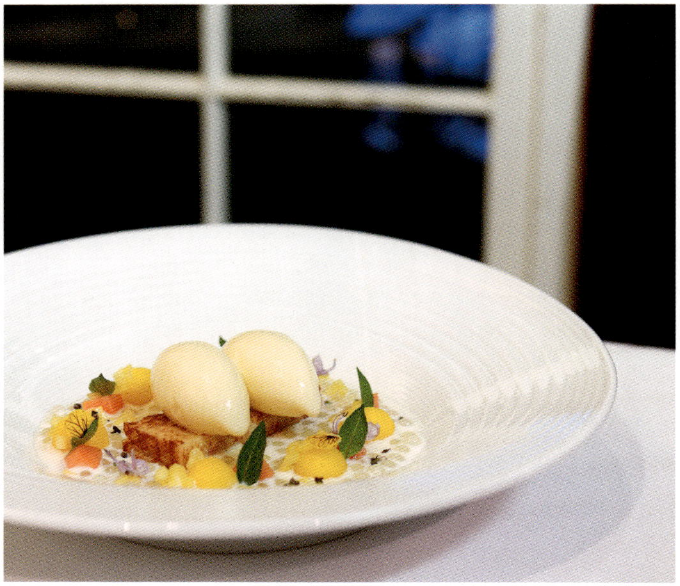

Saw the half-baguette into 1-inch slices and place them in a large mixing bowl with 4 cups of tap water. Let soak until soft, approximately 5-10 minutes.

In a blender, process the almonds, grapes, garlic, and mineral water until smooth—you may have to do this in 2 batches. Add the softened bread, olive oil, and vinegar to this mixture and process again until smooth. Pass the soup through a fine strainer and season with salt and pepper. Chill for 1 hour.

Garnish the soup with thinly sliced radishes, grapes, and toasted almonds.

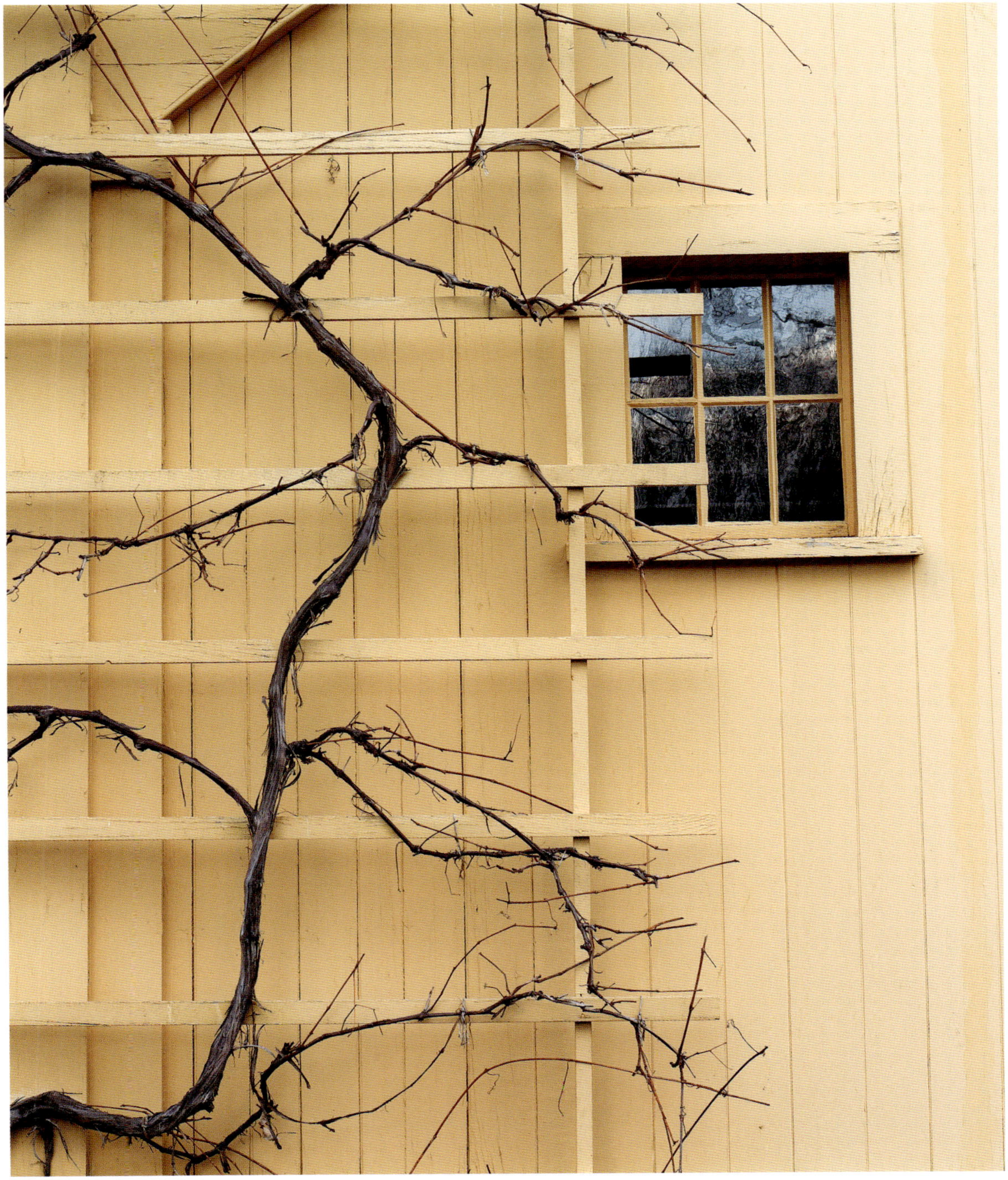

Salts Restaurant

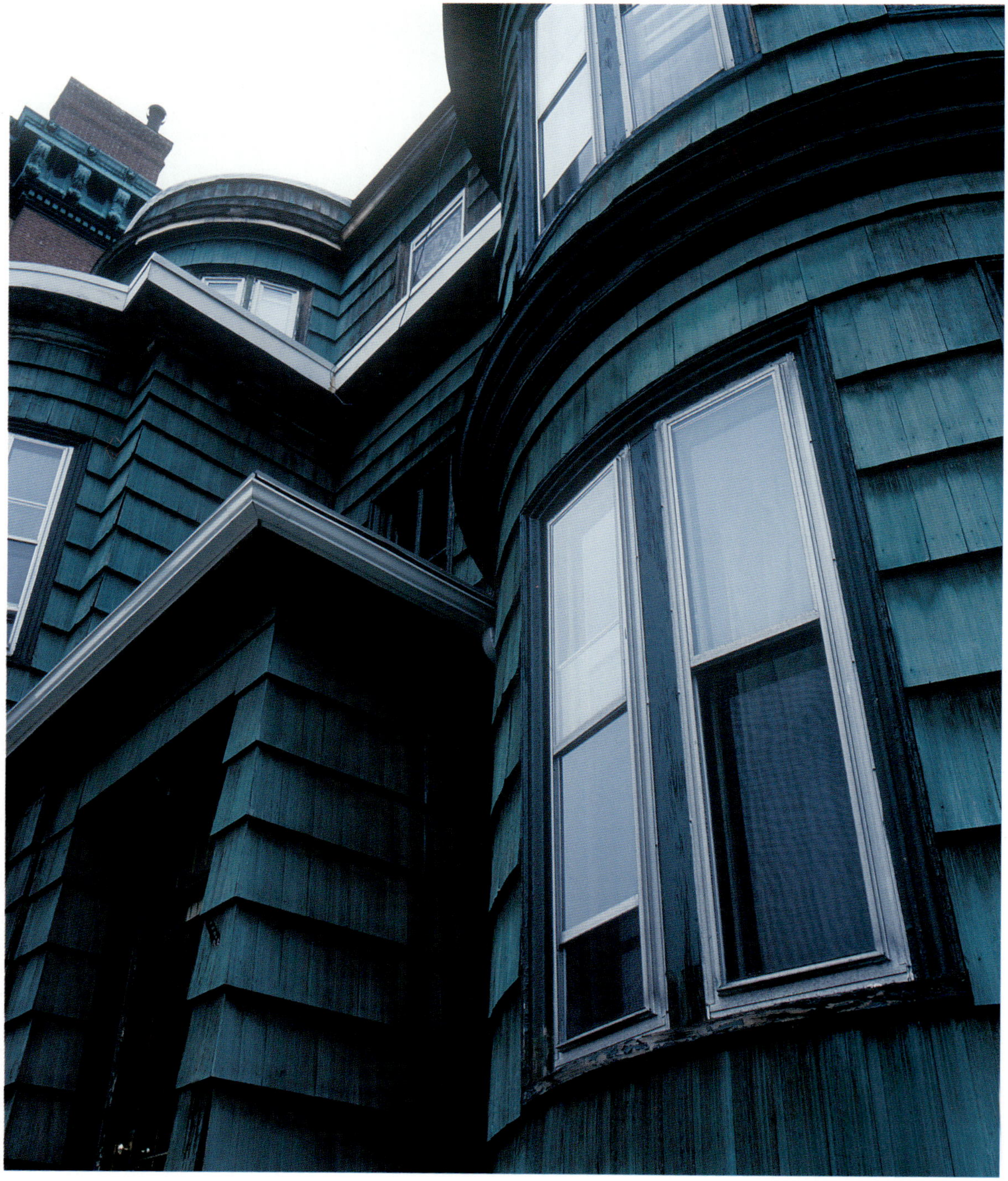

Casablanca

Seafood Stew

1 onion, julienne
6 bulbs garlic, smashed
2 teaspoons red pepper flakes
3 tablespoons chopped thyme
1 box Pom tomatoes, chopped
¼ cup diced Spanish chorizo

½ white onion, diced
½ cup Arborio rice

12 clams
12 large shrimp
4 ounces monkfish chunks
24 muscles
4 ounces fresh calamari, cut in rings
2 cups fume or chicken stock
¼ cup Parmesan cheese
2 tablespoons chopped parsley
4 tablespoons butter
¾ cup white wine

8 crostini

Serves 4

Spicy Tomato Sauce

In a wide saucepan, caramelize the onions and then add the thyme, garlic, red pepper flakes, and chorizo and cook until fragrant. Add the chopped tomatoes and simmer until very thick.

Risotto

In a separate pan, sauté the onion until tender and then add the rice, toasting slightly. Cover with water and cook until almost cooked through.

Heat a large pan until very hot and add the clams and white wine and cover immediately. Steam the clams until they begin to open. Add the fume or stock, spicy tomato sauce, and risotto and bring to a simmer. Add the rest of the ingredients and cook until the fish is cooked through and the muscles have opened. Season with salt and pepper and serve with the crostini.

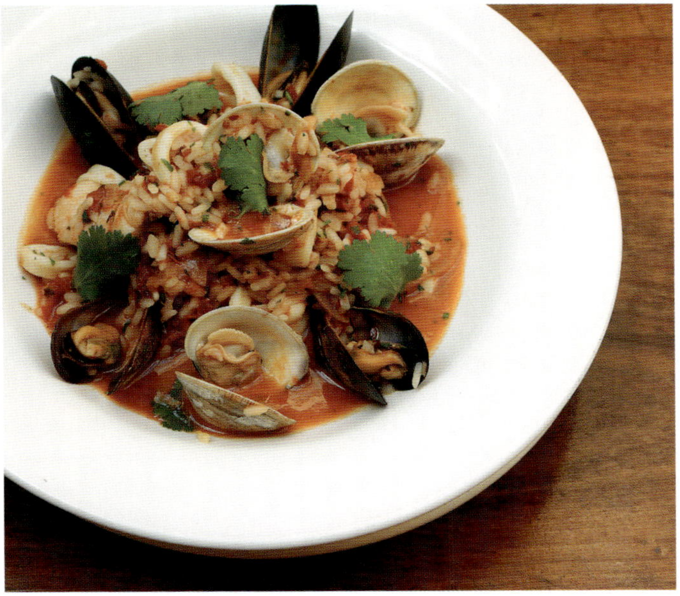

New England Clambake with Traditional Accompaniments

2 lobsters, 1½-2 pounds each
1 pound mussels, cleaned, beards removed
1 pound littleneck clams, cleaned
4 ears corn, shucked
½ pound fingerling potatoes, cooked in salted water until tender
1 bulb fennel with tops, bulb sliced, fronds removed and set aside
2 cups dry white wine
2 tablespoons unsalted butter
1 pound good-quality chorizo
Fresh lemon juice
Salt

Serves 4-6

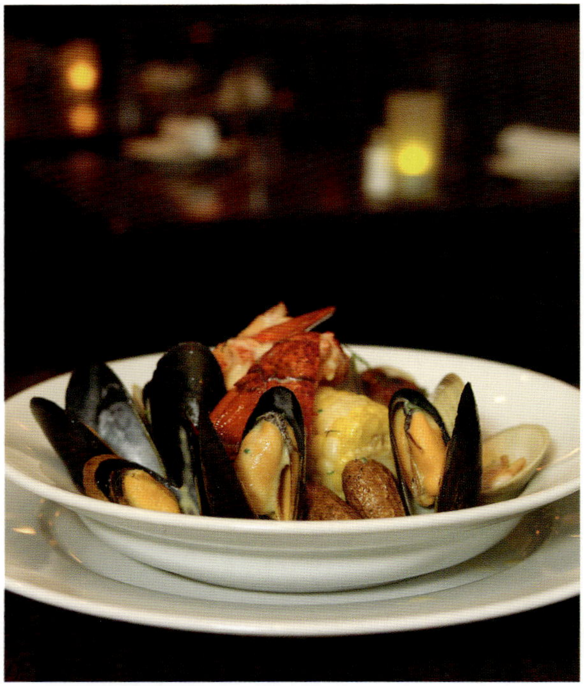

Place the lobsters in a large pot of boiling salted water and cook for 7 minutes. When cool enough to handle, remove the meat from the shells. In a large sauté pan with enough olive oil to cover the bottom, soften the sliced fennel bulb over medium heat. Add the littleneck clams and white wine and simmer, covered, until the clams begin to open. Add the mussels, potatoes, corn, and chorizo; cover and simmer until the mussels begin to open. Add the lobster meat and butter and season to taste with lemon and salt. Sprinkle some of the fennel fronds over the top and cover for 1 minute, until the butter has melted and the fennel fronds have wilted.

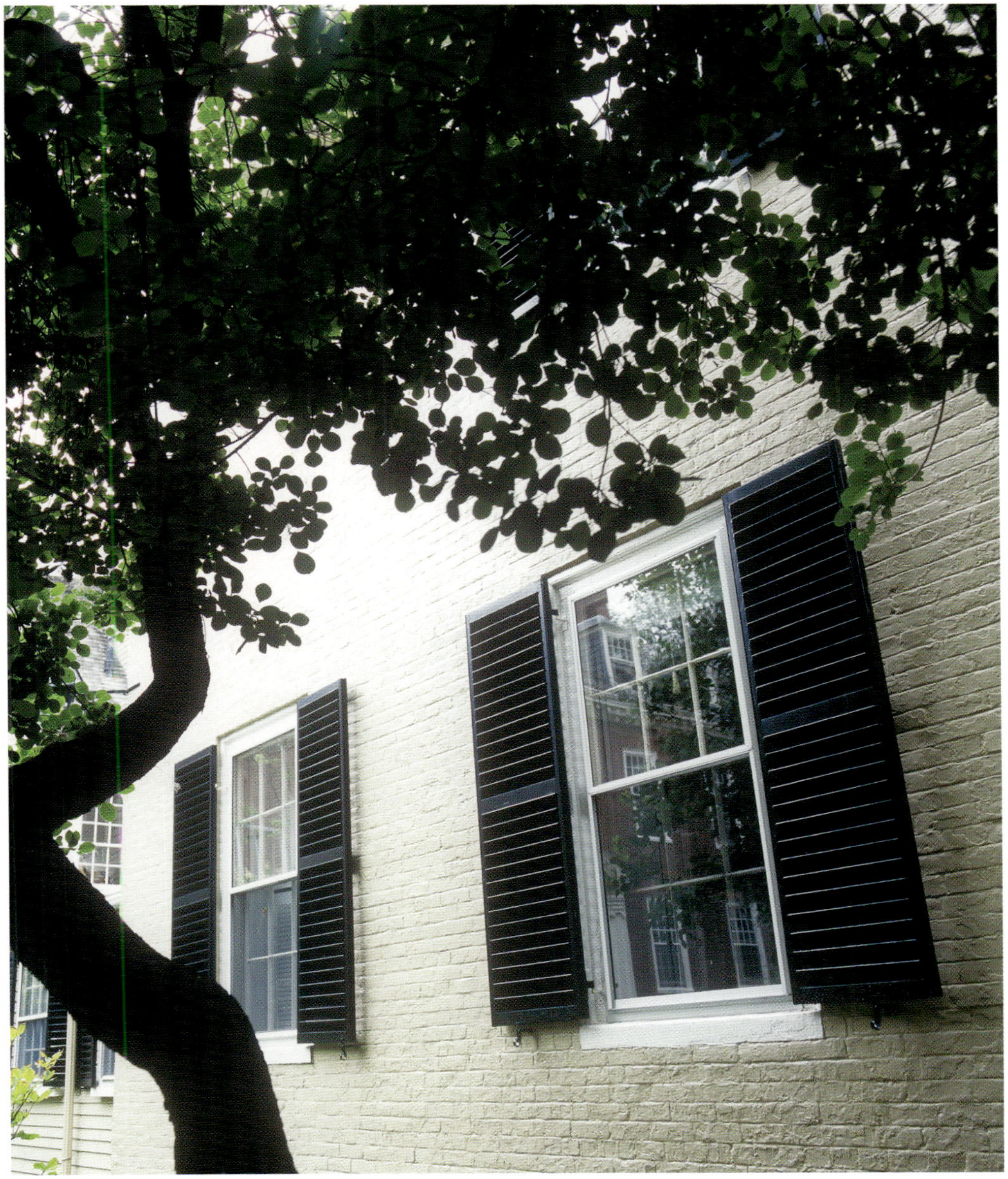

Green Street

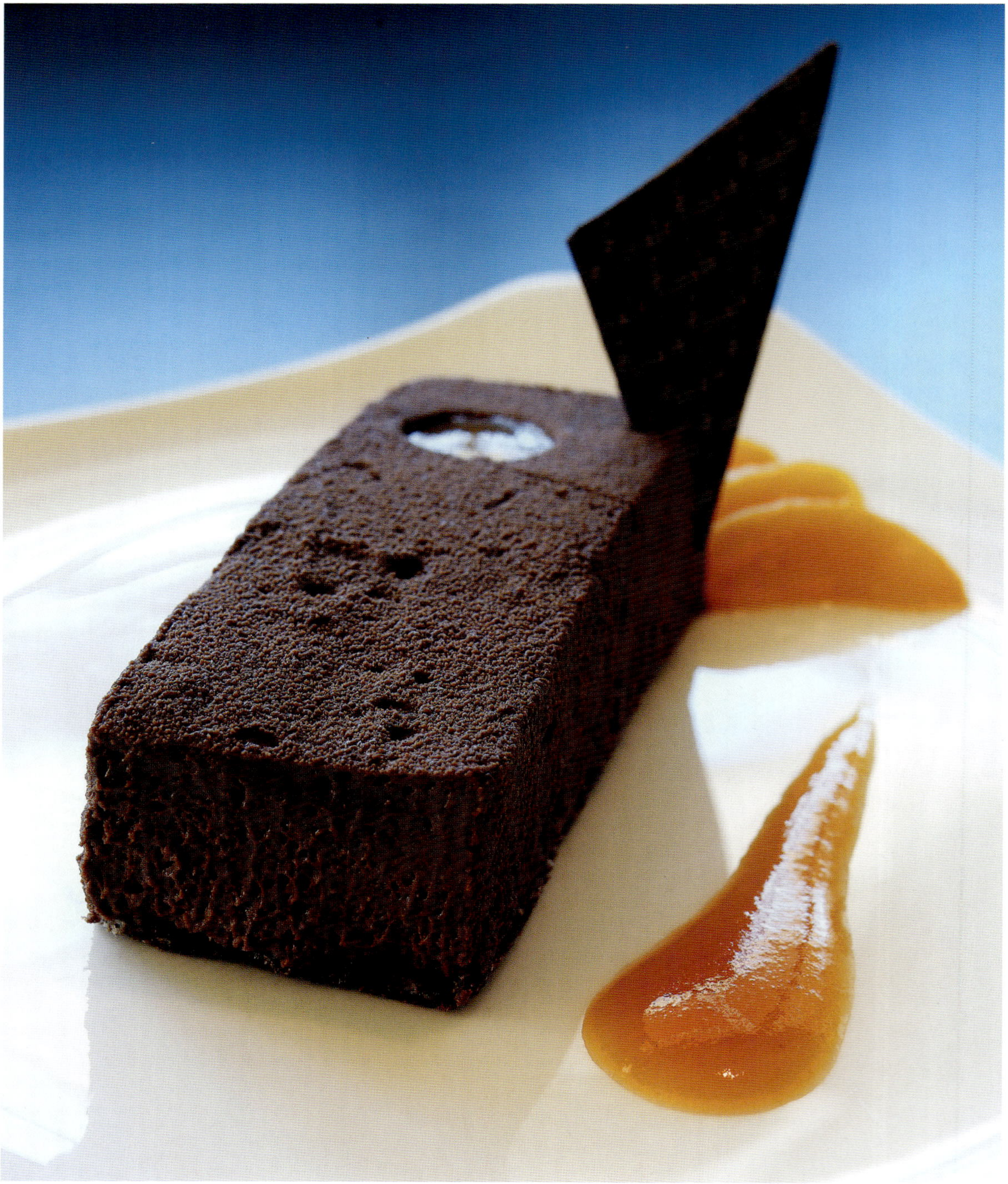

Bittersweet Chocolate Mousse with Apricot Sauce

Chocolate Mousse

12 ounces bittersweet chocolate, chopped
18 ounces heavy whipping cream
8 eggs separated, reserving yolks
2 eggs
1 cup granulated sugar
¼ cup water

Apricot Sauce

1 tablespoon cornstarch
3 ounces cold water
10 ounces apricot purée
2½ tablespoons corn syrup

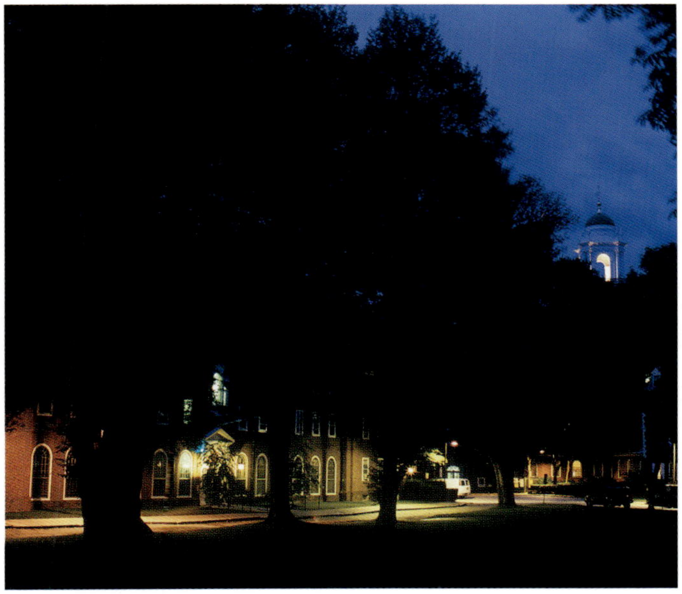

Chocolate Mousse

In a mixing bowl, using a mixer, whip cream until thick and reserve for later. Begin whipping whole eggs and yolks, and as they whip, heat the sugar and water to 240° using a candy thermometer. When the syrup reaches the correct temperature, slowly pour it into the whipped eggs. Whip sugar and eggs to about 6 times their original volume. While the eggs and sugar are whipping, place the chocolate in a microwave-safe bowl. Melt chocolate in short increments of time, stirring between each use of the microwave. When the chocolate is completely melted, slowly add it to the fully whipped eggs. Fold the whipped cream by hand into the chocolate and egg mixture. Serve immediately or chill, as desired.

Apricot Sauce

In a saucepot, bring the purée and corn syrup to a boil. While the puree is heating, dissolve the cornstarch in cold water; then add this to the boiling purée. Cook, stirring continuously, for at least 3 minutes. Allow to cool.

chapter three

Autumn

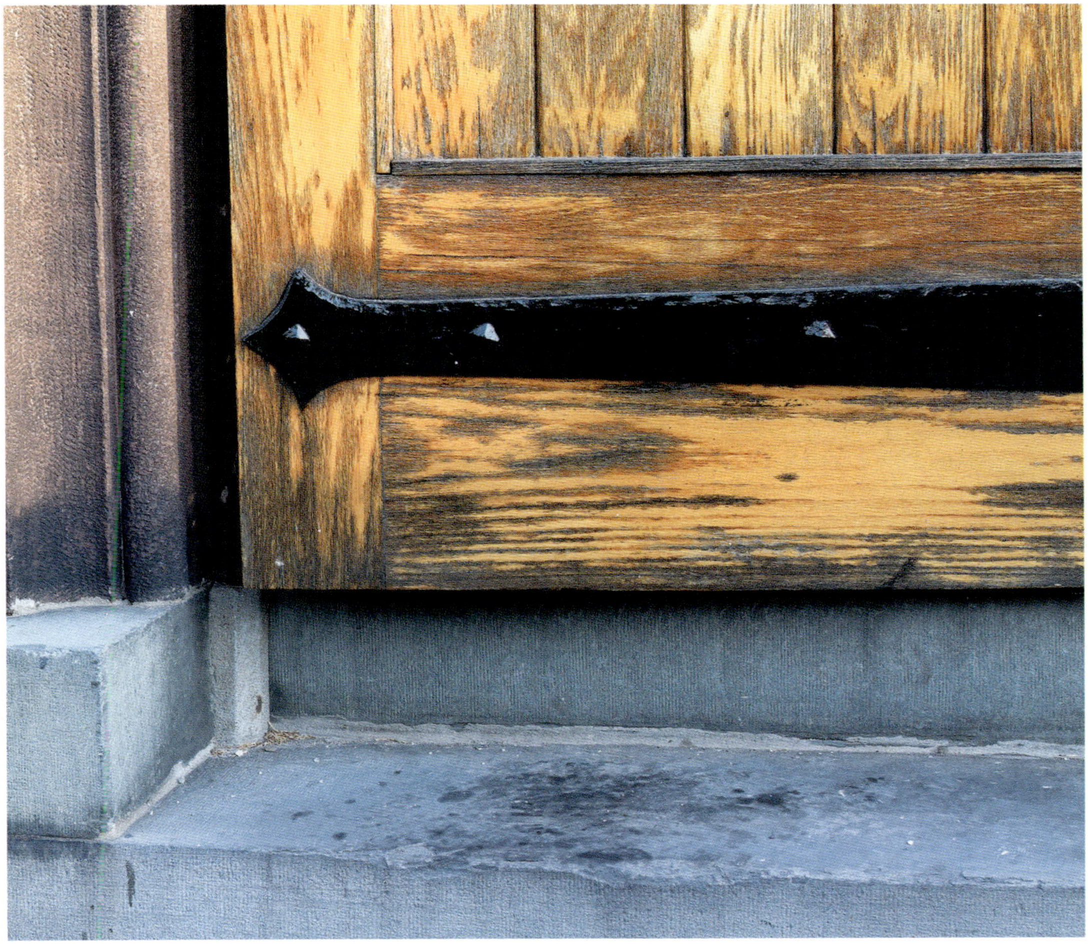

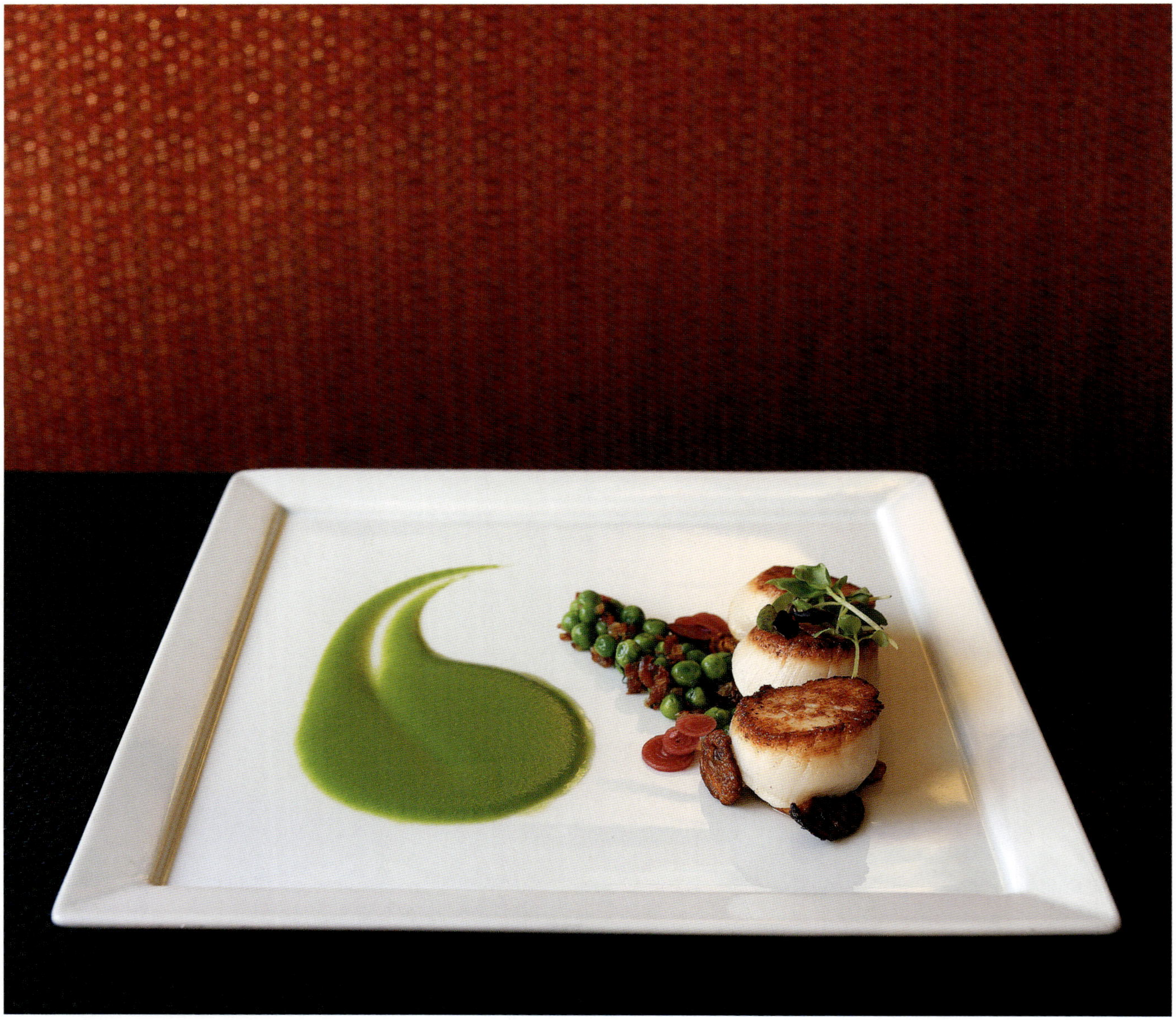

OM Restaurant

Pan-Roasted Scallops with Bacon and Ben's Mushrooms

Served with English Pea Purée and Pickled Pearl Onions

Scallops

30 U-10 dry sea scallops
¼ cup grapeseed oil
2 tablespoons unsalted butter
kosher salt
cracked pepper

Pea Purée

2 quarts frozen peas
water, as needed
1 cup basil, blanched
2 tablespoons fresh lemon juice, strained
1 tablespoon unsalted butter
kosher salt
granulated sugar

Mushroom Hash

1 cup portobello mushrooms, brunoise
1 cup Spanish onion, brunoise
2 cup slab bacon, brunoise
1½ tablespoons sugar

Pickled Pearl Onions

1 teaspoon fennel seeds
1 teaspoon cumin seeds
1 teaspoon mustard seeds
1 teaspoon black peppercorns
½ teaspoon red pepper flakes
1 bay leaf
1½ cups red wine vinegar
¼ cup granulated sugar
12 pearl onions, peeled, trimmed, and blanched
salt to taste

Serves 6

Clean scallops of side muscle, lay them out on a tray, and season with salt and pepper. Bring a nonreactive sauté pan up to high heat. Add grapeseed oil and when the oil ripples, place scallops in the pan, being careful not to overcrowd them. Let them cook in the pan until their bottoms turn golden brown. Add butter. Place the pan in the oven and cook until medium or desired temperature. Turn the scallops over and remove from pan.

Defrost the peas. Place 1 quart of peas in a blender and turn the blender on medium speed. Add water slowly to get peas moving. Add basil. Add more water if necessary. Turn blender up to high. Blend until smooth. Strain through a chinois. Season with salt and sugar. Place in a plastic container with a cover if serving later. To serve, place purée in a nonreactive saucepot and warm over low heat; the purée should never boil. Just before serving, add lemon juice and whisk in butter. Reseason with salt and sugar to taste.

In a sauté pan, render bacon. Remove bacon and toss with sugar. Sweat Spanish onion in bacon fat until golden brown and remove. Sauté portobello mushrooms and let cool. Mix all ingredients together and adjust seasoning. Before serving, heat mixture over medium heat. Blanch remaining quart of peas in hot water and strain. Add peas to bacon mixture. Add mint and basil.

Slice king oyster mushrooms lengthwise in ⅛-inch slices. Pour grapeseed oil in a sauté pan and bring the temperature up to high heat. Place mushrooms flat in the pan, being careful not to overcrowd them. Cook until golden-brown. Add butter, salt, and pepper. Baste with the butter. Remove from pan and drain on a towel.

Bring all ingredients except onions to a boil and simmer for 5 minutes. Pour over the onions and let cool. Let sit in pickling liquid for 2 days before serving. Slice in rounds before serving.

Pillows of Kuri Squash

Served with Meyer Lemon Fondue and Smoky Bacon

Ravioli Filling

1 kuri or butternut squash, cut in half lengthwise, seeds discarded
2 tablespoons kosher salt
1 teaspoon crushed red pepper
1 tablespoon butter
½ cup Parmesan cheese, grated
¼ nutmeg, grated on a microplane
1 egg

Pasta

4 cups all-purpose flour, plus extra for rolling out dough
1 teaspoon salt
4 eggs
1 tablespoon olive oil
egg wash—1 egg mixed with 1 tablespoon water

Finish

¼ pound bacon (double smoked is preferred), cut into ¼-inch cubes and cooked over low heat until crispy
4 tablespoons butter
2 tablespoons marjoram, chopped
1 Meyer lemon, segmented with the skin on and sliced thin

Ravioli Filling

Season the flesh of the squash with the red pepper flakes and 1 tablespoon of the salt; place the butter inside one of the halves. Close the two halves of the squash and wrap in foil. Bake at 350° until tender—about 45 minutes. Open the squash, careful not to burn yourself with the escaping steam, which builds up inside the cavity and helps with the cooking process. When the squash is room temperature, scoop the flesh into a bowl and discard the skin. Combine the remaining ingredients with the squash and mix thoroughly.

Pasta

Combine flour and salt on a clean table, create a well in the middle, and crack the eggs into it. Add olive oil and mix eggs and oil gently with a fork, being careful not to break the wall of flour. Slowly begin to incorporate the flour with the fork and bring the dough together. Knead for ten minutes, cover the dough with plastic wrap, and let rest at room temperature for half an hour. Cut the dough into quarters and roll out into thin sheets, cutting each sheet into squares that measure about two inches on each side. Place one teaspoon of the filling in the middle of each small square of pasta and paint the egg wash around it with your finger, being careful to go to the edge. Lift the corners to a point above the filling, and squeeze the sides of this "pyramid" together.

To Finish the Dish

Drop the ravioli into boiling salted water and cook until tender, approximately 2 minutes. Melt the butter in a sauté pan, add the marjoram and lemon, and season with salt. Add the ravioli to this mixture, then add the bacon, toss, and serve. Top with fresh herbs or Parmesan curls.

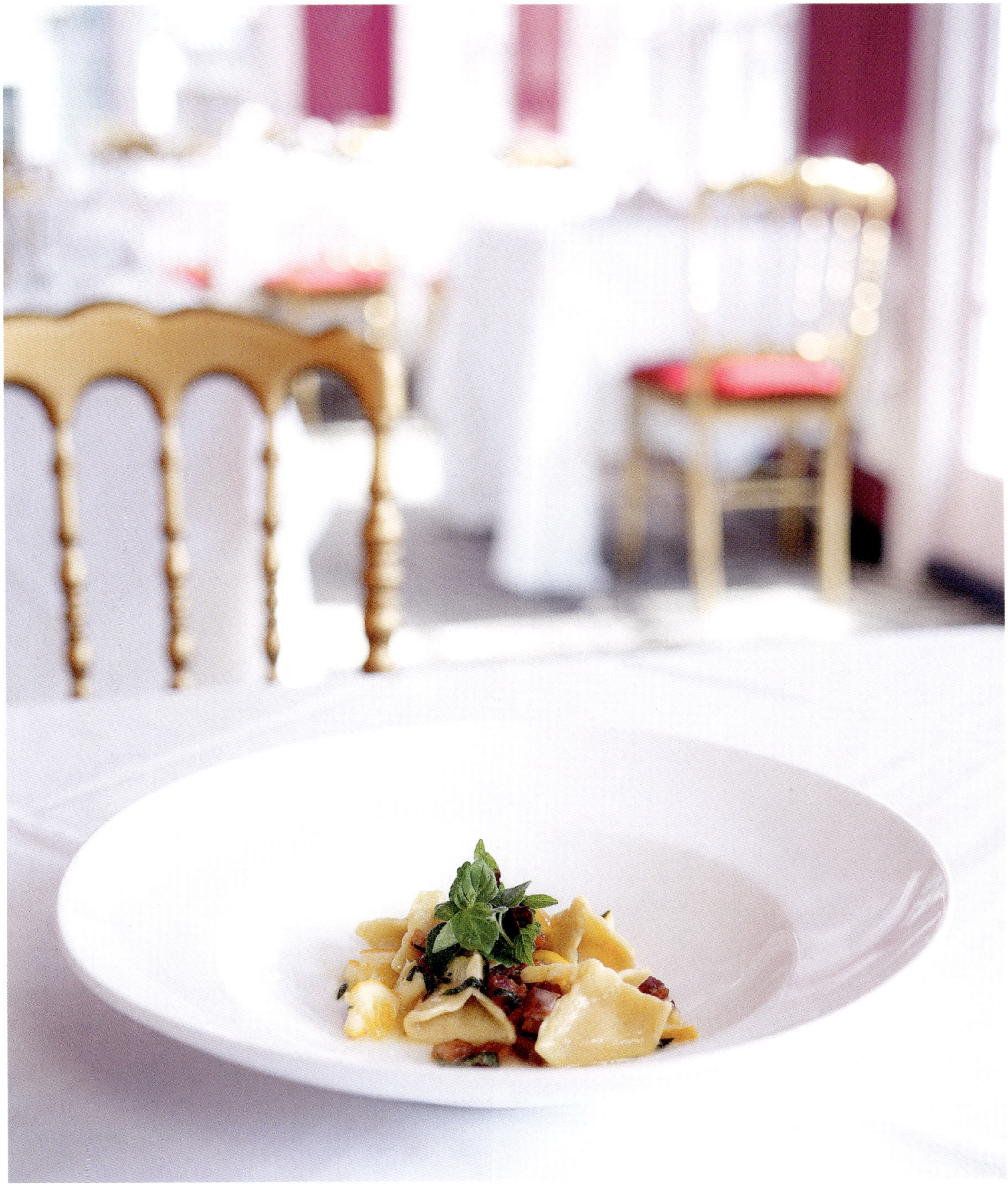

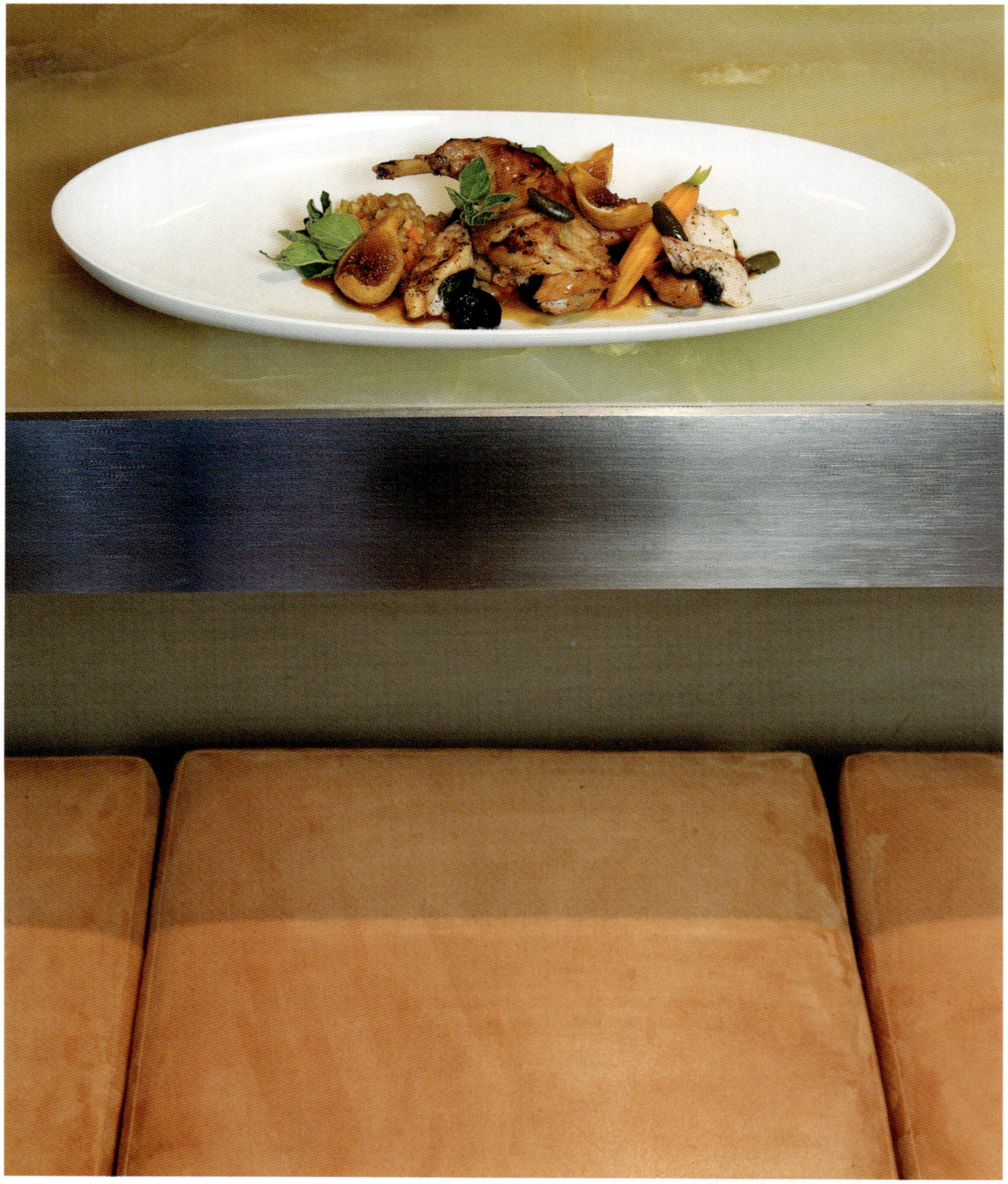

Braised Rabbit with Figs and Olives

Rialto

2 rabbits, about 3 pounds each, broken down in the following way: loins removed and trimmed of silver skin, forearms and hind legs removed, and carcass used for stock
Kosher salt and freshly ground black pepper
3 tablespoons vegetable oil
1 small parsnip, peeled and cut into ½-inch dice (if parsnips are unavailable, use a carrot)
1 small onion, cut into ½-inch dice
½ celery stalk, peeled and cut into ½-inch dice
2 garlic cloves, smashed and peeled
1 cup white wine
2 cups chicken stock
1 ½-inch strip lemon zest
1 sprig sage
2 bay leaves
2 tablespoons unsalted butter
16 Lucques olives, pitted and sliced
4 dried Turkish figs, soaked in hot water and quartered
12 baby carrots, peeled and blanched until tender
1 tablespoon balsamic vinegar
¼ teaspoon finely grated lemon zest
2 tablespoons oregano leaves
4 sprigs oregano for garnish

Season rabbit forearms and hind legs with salt and pepper. Heat the oil in a large sauté pan with 2-inch sides over medium heat. Brown the rabbit pieces on all sides. Transfer the rabbit pieces to a plate.

Add the parsnip or carrot, onion, celery, and garlic to the pan, season with salt and pepper, and cook, stirring often, until they begin to brown, about 5 minutes. Add the wine and reduce by half. Add the chicken stock, lemon zest, sage, and bay leaves and reduce by half again. Reduce the heat to the lowest setting so the liquid is just simmering.

Return the rabbit pieces to the pan, cover with a parchment round and a lid, and cook 30-45 minutes or until the rabbit is very tender. Remove the rabbit pieces and reduce the juices until they will coat the back of a spoon. Remove and discard the lemon zest, sage sprig, and bay leaves. Return the rabbit pieces to the juices and keep warm.

Cut each loin into 4 pieces. Season with salt and pepper. Heat the butter till it foams in a large sauté pan over medium heat. When the foam subsides, add the loin pieces and cook until brown on all sides and cooked through, about 5 minutes. Add the olives, figs, and carrots and toss well until heated through. Add the balsamic vinegar, lemon zest, and oregano leaves and toss again.

To serve, arrange a forearm and hind leg on each of 4 warm plates. Spoon the loin mixture over the legs and then a spoonful of the braising juices. Garnish with oregano sprigs and serve immediately.

Scallop Carpaccio

10 large scallops
6 red peppers
12 pink peppercorns
1 chive flower
10 oyster mushrooms
olive oil
champagne vinegar

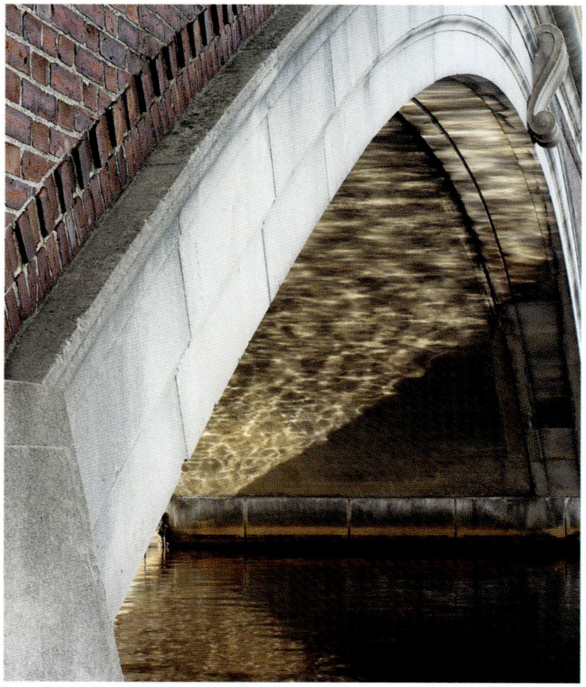

Served with Red Pepper Marmelade and Pickled Mushroom

Peel the peppers, remove the seeds and ribs, and slice very fine. Cook over low heat with olive oil until very soft. Cool. Slice the mushrooms and sauté, then deglaze with 2 tablespoons vinegar and olive oil. Season and cool. Slice the scallops paper-thin and arrange in a circle. Garnish with the marmelade and arrange the pickled mushrooms around the scallops.

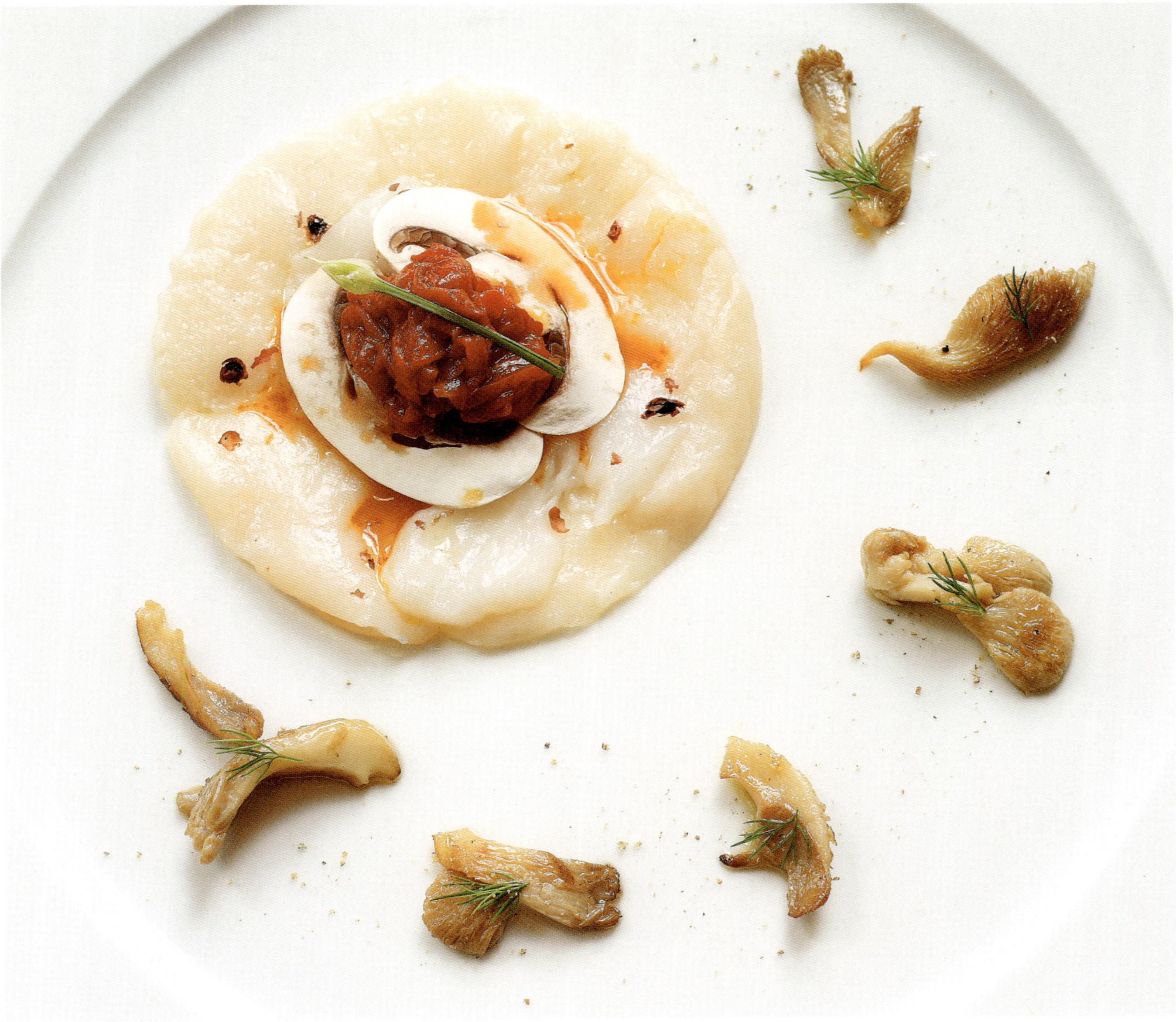

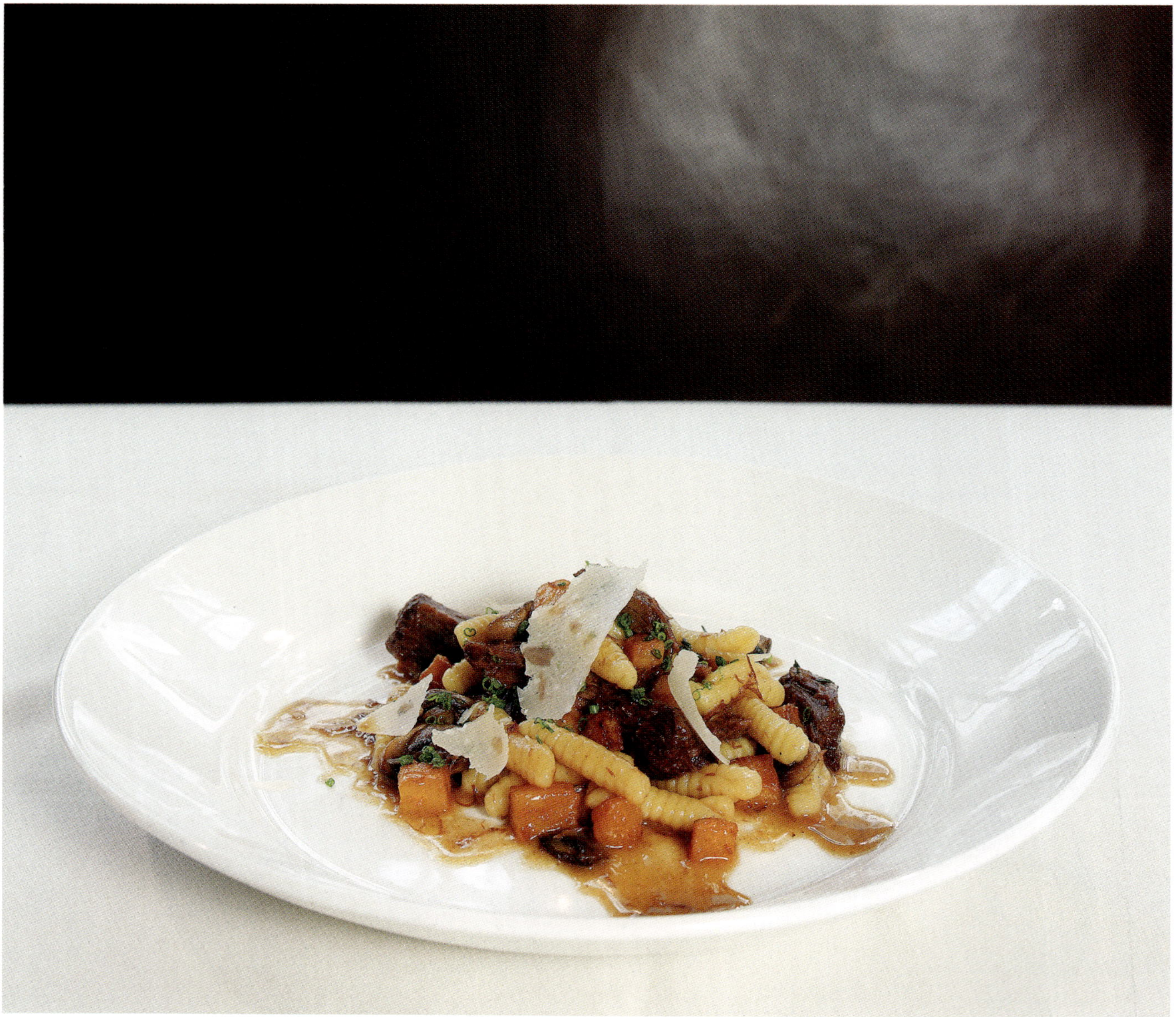

Braised Oxtail Cavatelli with Butternut Squash

Served with Fancy Mushrooms and White Truffle Butter

Braised Oxtail

2 pounds oxtail
salt and pepper to taste
2 tablespoons olive oil
1 large onion, chopped
1 large carrot, chopped
1 rib celery, chopped
½ head garlic
¼ gallon chicken stock

Butternut Squash Dice

3 tablespoons canola oil
½ cup butternut squash, diced
salt to taste

Mushroom Stock

¼ pound porcini mushrooms, dried
1 quart filtered water

Cavatelli Sauce

3 cups mushroom stock
1 cup oxtail braising liquid

Cavatelli Pasta

1 tablespoon duck fat
2 egg yolks
4 cups extra-fine semolina flour
1 teaspoon salt
1 cup water

Additional Ingredients

1 tablespoon butter
2 cups fancy mushrooms, sliced thick
1 teaspoon minced shallot
1 teaspoon chopped garlic
3 tablespoons white truffle butter
½ cup Parmesan grated cheese
⅛ cup chopped chives

Serves 8

Season the oxtails liberally with salt and pepper. Heat 1 tablespoon of the olive oil in a large roasting pan and sear each side of each oxtail. Remove from heat, and trim any excess fat. Heat the remaining olive oil and sauté the vegetables until they caramelize, approximately 5 minutes. Return the meat to the pan and add the chicken stock. Bring to a boil, cover the pan, and place it in the oven for 3 hours. Remove the cover and cook for an additional 30 minutes. Remove from heat and allow to cool. Pick the meat from the bones and set aside. Strain the liquid and reserve.

Heat the oil in a sauté pan over high heat. Add the butternut squash and sauté until golden brown. Stir the squash minimally as it caramelizes to retain its texture. Remove squash from the pan and allow it to dry on paper towels. Season with salt and set aside.

Place mushrooms and water in a pot and bring to a boil. Lower the heat and allow the stock to steep for 45 minutes. Strain through a chinois and allow to cool; set aside.

Combine the liquids in a small saucepot and bring to a boil. Remove from heat and strain through a chinois. Allow the sauce to cool in an ice bath.

Mix the duck fat and egg yolks together, blending until smooth. Add the dry ingredients and mix until well incorporated. Add the water and blend until smooth. Allow the dough to rest for 1 hour, then roll it out on a dry, lightly floured surface to ¾-inch thickness. Cut the dough into 1/2-inch wide strips, and roll it through a cavatelli pasta maker, according to the manufacturer's instructions. Cook the cavatelli in a large pot of salted boiling water for 4 minutes. Strain and immediately shock the pasta in an ice bath. When the pasta has cooled, remove it from the ice water and allow to dry.

Heat the butter in a large pan and brown the mushrooms over high heat. Add the shallots and garlic and sauté until fragrant. Reduce the heat to medium and add the oxtail meat, squash, 1 quart of cavatelli pasta, and 4 cups of cavatelli sauce. Reduce the mixture until the sauce is noticeably clinging to the pasta. Add the truffle butter and Parmesan cheese. Salt and pepper to taste. Divide the pasta among heated serving plates. Garnish each dish with chives and serve immediately.

Harvard Square

3 sticks unsalted butter
2 pounds high-quality dark chocolate
8 eggs
1½ teaspoons salt
4 cups sugar
1 vanilla bean
1 pound toasted walnuts
¾ cup flour

Ganache

1½ pounds high-quality dark chocolate
3 cups heavy cream
splash of rum, optional

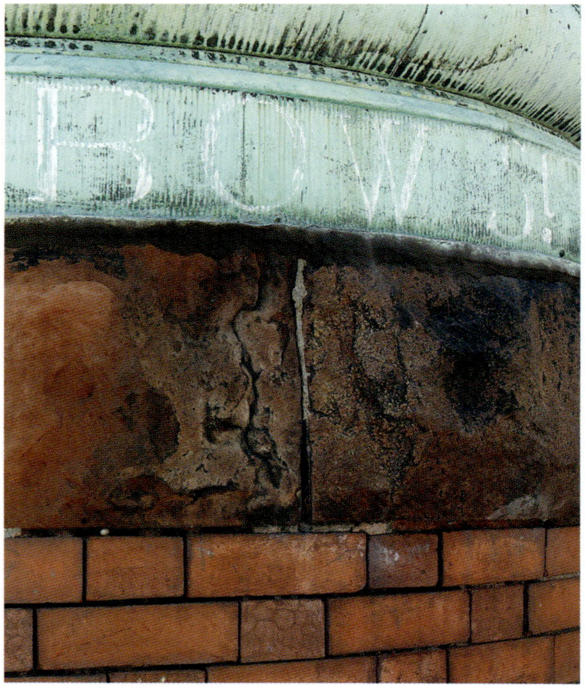

Melt chocolate and butter over a double boiler. Mix eggs, salt, sugar, and vanilla bean for 10 minutes, then add chocolate and butter mixture. Add walnuts, then flour, until combined. Spread on a buttered 9-x-3-inch pan and bake at 325° for 25 minutes. Let cool.

For the Ganache

Heat cream and pour over chocolate. Whisk until chocolate is melted. Add rum. Pour over cake and chill. Cut into squares and serve.

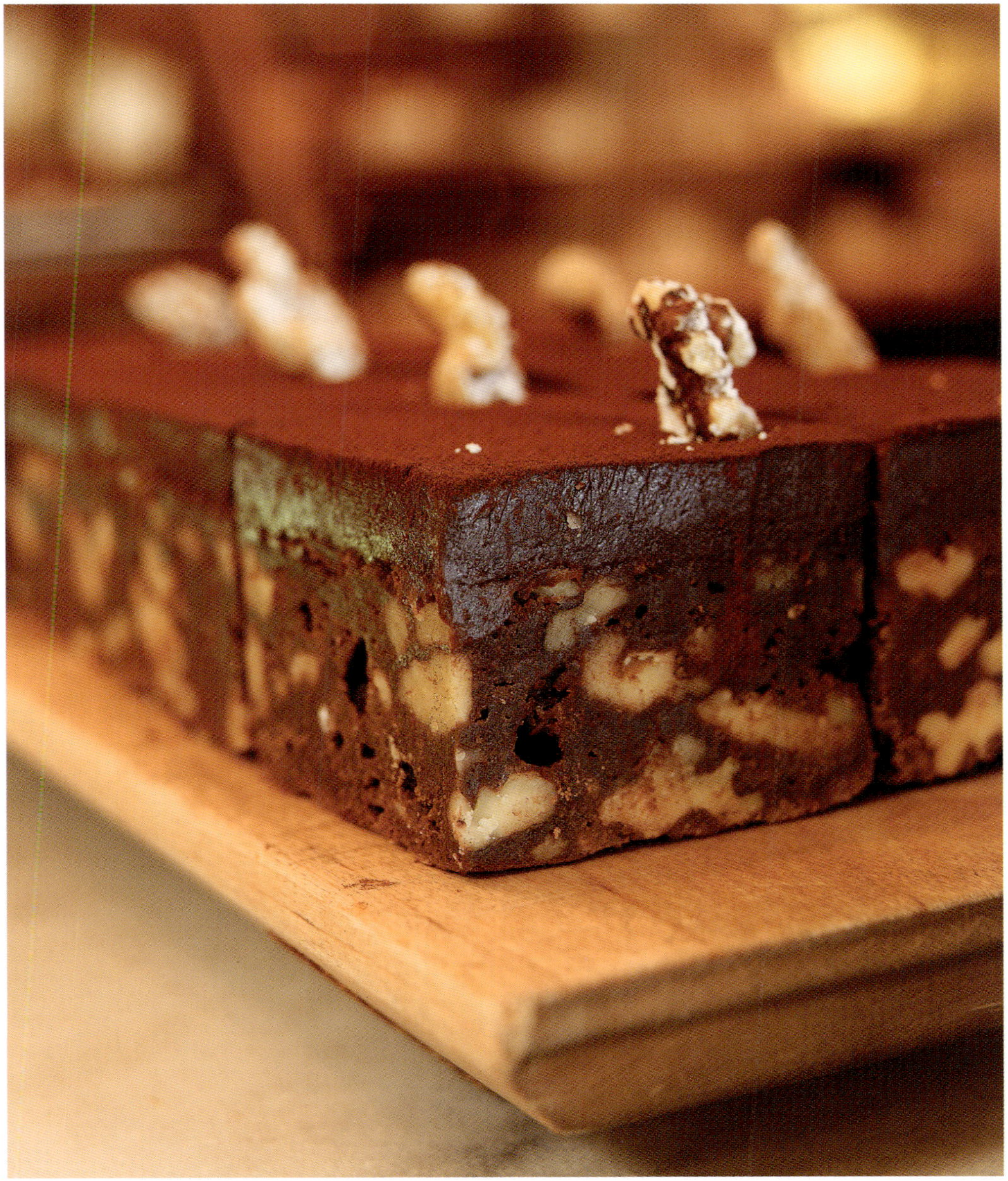

L.A. Burdick

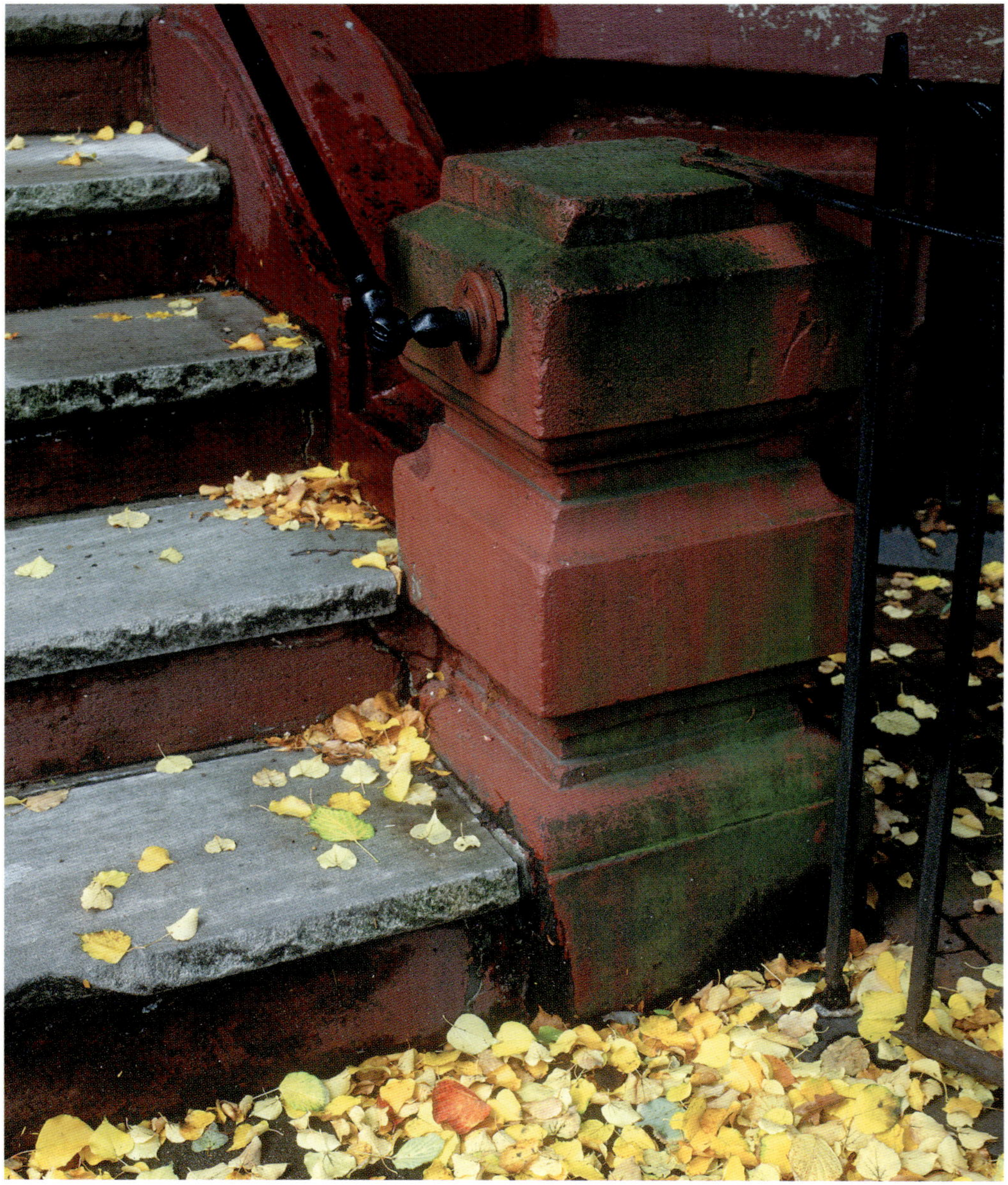

Salts Farm Heirloom Tomatoes

Tomato "Tart Tatin"

4 small-medium heirloom tomatoes, as round as possible
4 rounds puff pastry, 2½ inches in diameter
1 cup sherry vinegar
¼ cup sugar
1 tablespoon butter
sea salt

Tomato Consommé

2 pounds heirloom tomatoes
12 red and yellow cherry tomatoes, blanched and peeled
sea salt
cheesecloth

Grilled Cheese and Tomato Sandwich with Summer Truffle

4 slices of brioche or good-quality white bread
Robiola cheese
1 heirloom tomato, thinly sliced
1 black summer truffle, thinly shaved, optional
2 tablespoons butter

Simple Salad of Heirloom Tomatoes

4 assorted heirloom tomatoes, such as green zebra, brandy wine, and pine
good-quality fruity olive oil (Spanish preferred)
sea salt

Serves 4

Tomato "Tart Tatin"

Combine the sherry vinegar and sugar in a pot and reduce over a low flame until you achieve a caramel-like consistency. Whisk in the butter and pour the caramel into 4 ovenproof ramekins. Slice off the tops of the tomatoes and place them, cut side up, in the ramekins. Season with salt and pepper and top with the rounds of puff pastry. Bake at 375° until golden-brown, about 30 minutes.

Consommé of Heirloom Tomato

Chop the tomatoes and place them in a large mixing bowl with 1 tablespoon of coarse sea salt. Let sit for 10 minutes. Line the inside of a large strainer or colander with cheesecloth and place in another large bowl. Pour the tomatoes into the lined strainer and let sit. After about 1 hour, the bowl will be filled with a clear tomato consommé.

Grilled Cheese

Top 2 slices of the brioche with the robiola cheese, thinly sliced tomato, and shavings of black truffle. Close the sandwiches and place them in a sauté pan over a medium-low flame, dividing the butter and grilling until golden-brown on both sides.

Tomato Salad

Slice the tomatoes into ¼-inch slices and place them in a baking dish. Season with sea salt and drizzle with 5 tablespoons of olive oil. Let them sit for 30 minutes before serving. After 30 minutes, the tomatoes will have created their own perfect vinaigrette.

To Serve

On a large plate, place a few slices of tomato and dress them with their juices. Next to the salad, place a small glass filled with tomato consommé, garnished with several cherry tomatoes. Finish the plate with ½ hot grilled cheese sandwich and a tarte hot from the oven.

Salmon Ceviche, Crispy Sushi Rice Cake, and Lilikoi Vinaigrette

Lilikoi Vinaigrette

1 stick, unsalted butter
8 ounces lilikoi (passion fruit) purée
1 tablespoon Dijon mustard
½ shallot sliced
2 tablespoons sugar
kosher salt

Sushi Rice Cakes

3 cups short-grain Japanese rice
2½ cups cold water
3 ounces rice wine vinegar
1 tablespoon sugar
1 tablespoon mirin
canola oil for cooking

Ceviche

2 cups very fresh salmon, diced into small cubes
juice of 2-3 limes
1 tablespoon chili oil
3 scallions, sliced thin, green parts only
kosher salt and freshly ground black pepper

Fried Taro

½ cup thinly sliced match sticks of taro root
canola oil for frying

Serves 4-6

Lilikoi Vinaigrette

Gently brown the butter in a small pan over medium heat—approximately 10 minutes. While the butter is browning add the puree, Dijon, shallot, and sugar to a blender and purée smooth. When the butter is lightly browned and nutty smelling, pour all at once into the lilikoi mixture, being careful not to let it boil over. Season with salt and purée until emulsified.

Sushi Rice Cakes

Rinse the rice 3-4 times and strain. Combine the water and rice in a small sauce pot and cover tightly. Cook over medium heat for 15 minutes. Let rest for an additional 15 minutes. Do not uncover the rice during cooking or resting. In a small pan, gently heat the vinegar, sugar, and mirin until dissolved. Fold the vinegar mixture into the rice, cover with a damp towel and let cool to room temperature. Using a 3-inch ring mold, form 4 rice cakes about 2 inches thick. Coat the bottom of a sauté pan with canola oil over medium heat and sear the rice cakes on one side until golden, about three minutes.

Ceviche

Just before serving, toss the salmon, lime juice, chili oil and scallions in a nonreactive bowl. Season very well with salt and freshly ground black pepper.

Fried Taro

Soak the sliced taro in hot tap water for 10 minutes. In a deep pot, heat 3 inches of canola oil to 325°. Drain the taro and fry for 1-2 minutes until golden and crispy. Drain on a towel and season with salt.

Plating

Place the rice cakes seared side down on four plates. Divide the ceviche neatly onto the rice cakes, and drizzle the lilikoi sauce around the plate. Garnish with the fried taro root and a drizzle of extra chili oil.

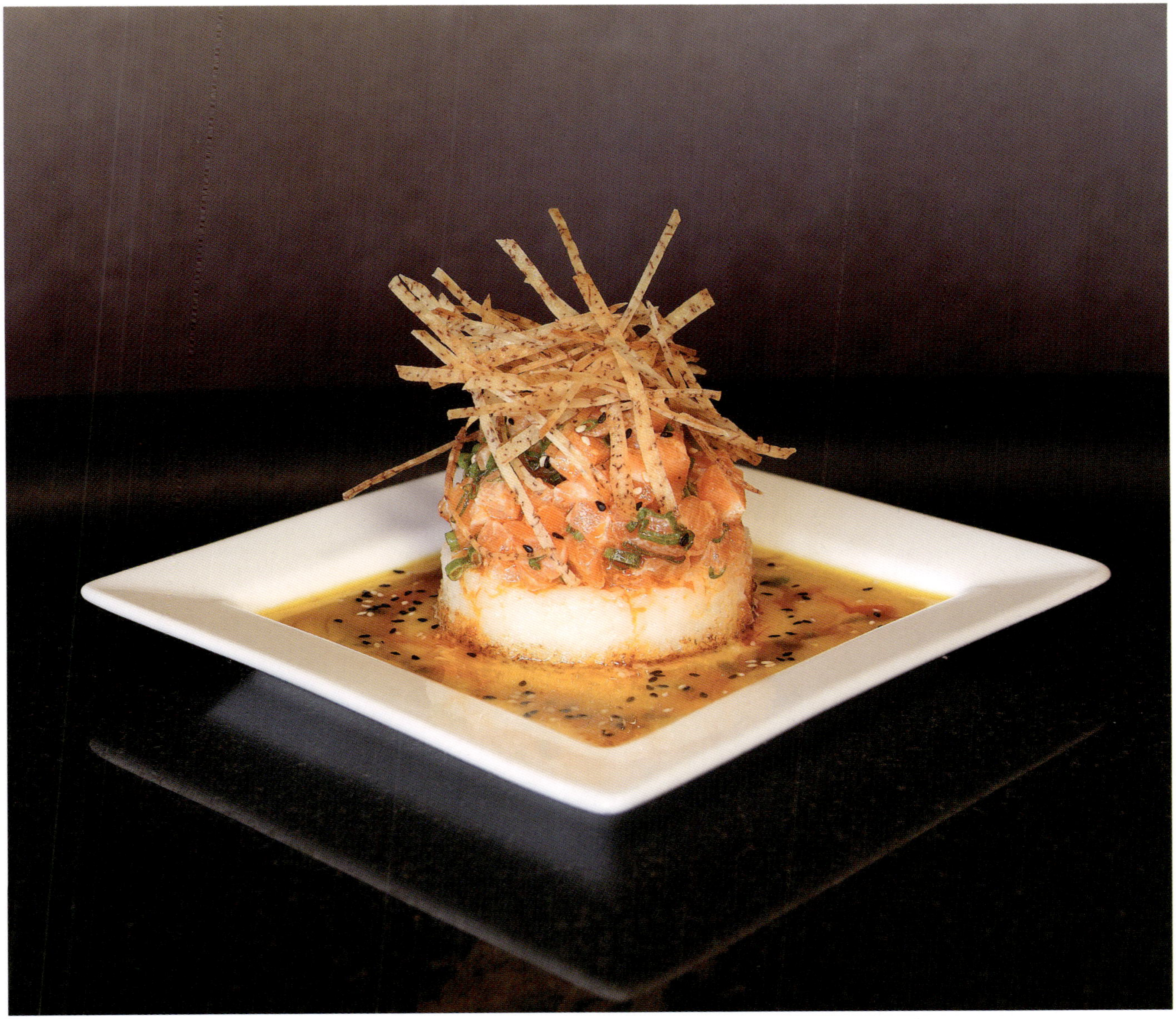

TEMPLE BAR

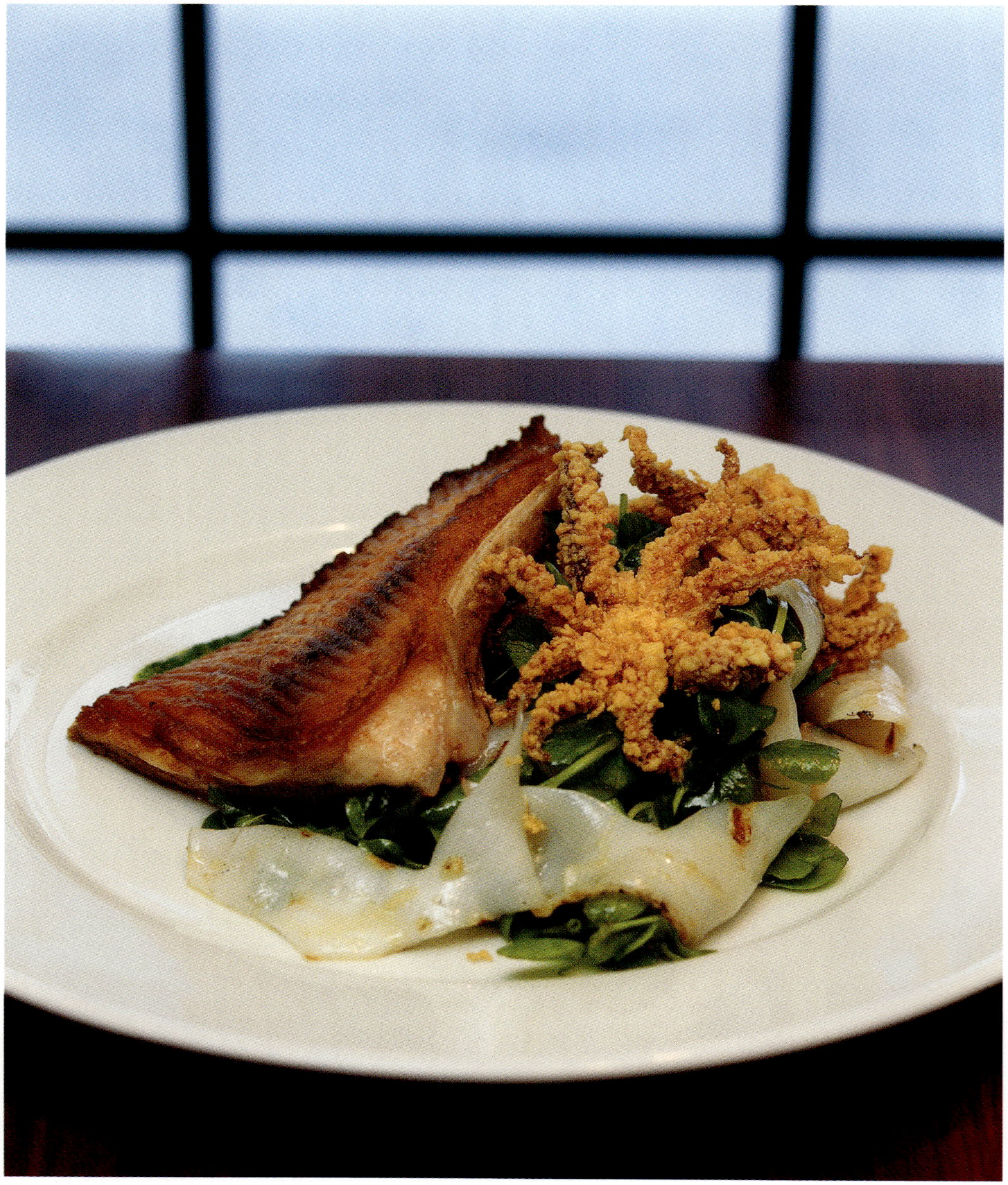

Pan-Roasted Skate Wing

Served with Scalloped Potatoes, Grilled Squid, and Pea Greens

2 pounds skate wing on the bone
6 large Yukon Gold potatoes
5 shallots
2 leeks
1 cup grated Parmesan cheese
10 sprigs thyme, stems removed
1 pint heavy cream
½ pound fresh squid, tubes and tentacles, cleaned
½ pound young pea greens

Serves 4-6

Skate Wing

Cut the skate into as many pieces as guests you are serving (or have your fish monger do this for you). In a very hot sauté pan with enough oil to cover the bottom, sear the skate until it is golden-brown on one side, flip it over, and place it in a 425° oven until the flesh is easily removed from the bone.

Scalloped Potatoes

Slice the potatoes on a mandolin, a little less than ¼-inch thick. Submerge in cold water to prevent oxidation. Slice the leeks and shallots very thin on the mandolin. Cover the bottom of a large baking dish with a small amount of the heavy cream. Overlapping the potatoes, make one layer in the baking dish. Evenly distribute ¼ of the leeks, shallots, cheese, and thyme and season with salt and pepper. Repeat this process until you have filled the baking dish. Cover the dish with aluminum foil and bake at 425° for about 2 hours, or until the potatoes are very tender.

Salad

Season the squid with salt and pepper and grill very quickly, until the bodies begin to curl at the edges. Remove from the grill and cut into bite-sized pieces. Toss the squid with the pea greens, lemon juice, olive oil, and salt.

Green Gnocchi with Spring Vegetables

Gnocchi

1 pound baking potatoes, scrubbed
1 pound fresh spinach, washed and trimmed of stems (baby spinach works well)
Salt to taste
½ cup ricotta cheese, drained
1 extra-large egg, beaten
½ cup grated Parmesan cheese
Freshly ground black pepper
¾ cup all-purpose flour
4 tablespoons unsalted butter

Spring Vegetables and Sauce

½ cup diagonally-cut asparagus
¼ cup baby carrot slices—they should be paper-thin and cut on the bias
¼ cup sliced scallions
¾ cup fresh peas
1 cup chicken stock
4 tablespoons unsalted butter
2 tablespoons chopped fresh herbs such as parsley, mint, basil, chervil, and savory
1 teaspoon lemon juice
Salt and freshly ground black pepper
2 ounces freshly shaved Parmesan cheese

Serves 4

Gnocchi

Preheat the oven to 400°. Roast the potatoes 1 hour, or until tender. While the potatoes are still warm, cut them in half and scoop the potato out of the skin and force through a ricer or sieve—if you wait until the potatoes are cool, they will be gummy.

Meanwhile, put the spinach in a large pot, sprinkle with salt, cover, and cook over medium-high heat in the water that clings to the leaves from washing, until the spinach has wilted. Drain in a colander, and when cool enough to handle, use your hands to squeeze out all the water, pressing the spinach against the sides of the colander or wringing it out in a clean towel. Chop the leaves as finely as possible with a knife—do not put in a food processor, or the spinach will become too wet. In a large bowl, mix the spinach with the ricotta and egg. Add the potato and ¼ cup of the Parmesan cheese and season with salt and pepper. Fold in the flour, then turn the mixture onto a floured counter and knead until smooth and slightly elastic, 1 to 2 minutes.

Roll the dough in a log about ½ inch in diameter—you may need to divide the dough into 2-3 logs, depending on the length of your countertop. Cut the logs into ½-inch pieces. Dust with flour so the gnocchi don't stick together. Form a depression in the center with your finger or roll the gnocchi with a fork to form a pattern.

Bring a large pot of water to a boil. Season with salt. Add the gnocchi and cook at a gentle boil until the gnocchi float to the surface, 5 minutes or less. With a slotted spoon, scoop out the gnocchi and toss with melted butter and the remaining ¼ cup of grated Parmesan. Place roughly 12 gnocchi in each serving bowl, cover with sauce, top with shaved cheese, and serve immediately with spring vegetables.

Spring Vegetables and Sauce

Bring a large pot of water to a boil. Season with salt. Add the asparagus, carrots, scallions, and peas. Drain and plunge into ice water to stop the cooking. Drain again. Bring the chicken stock to a boil over high heat, reduce the heat to low, and let it reduce by ½. Whisk in the butter, a little at a time, until well incorporated. Add the blanched vegetables, herbs, and lemon juice and heat through. Season with salt and pepper.

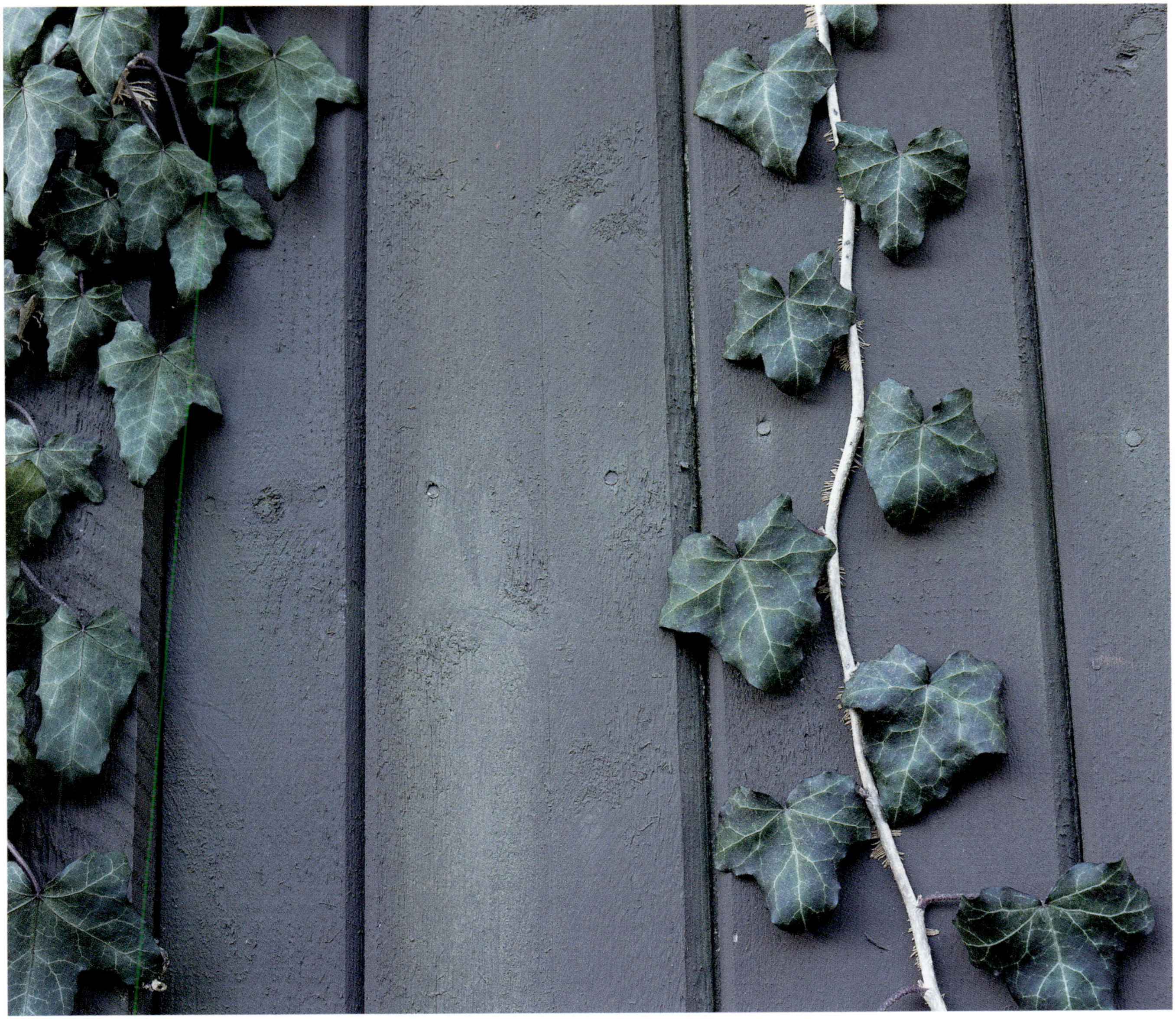

Rialto

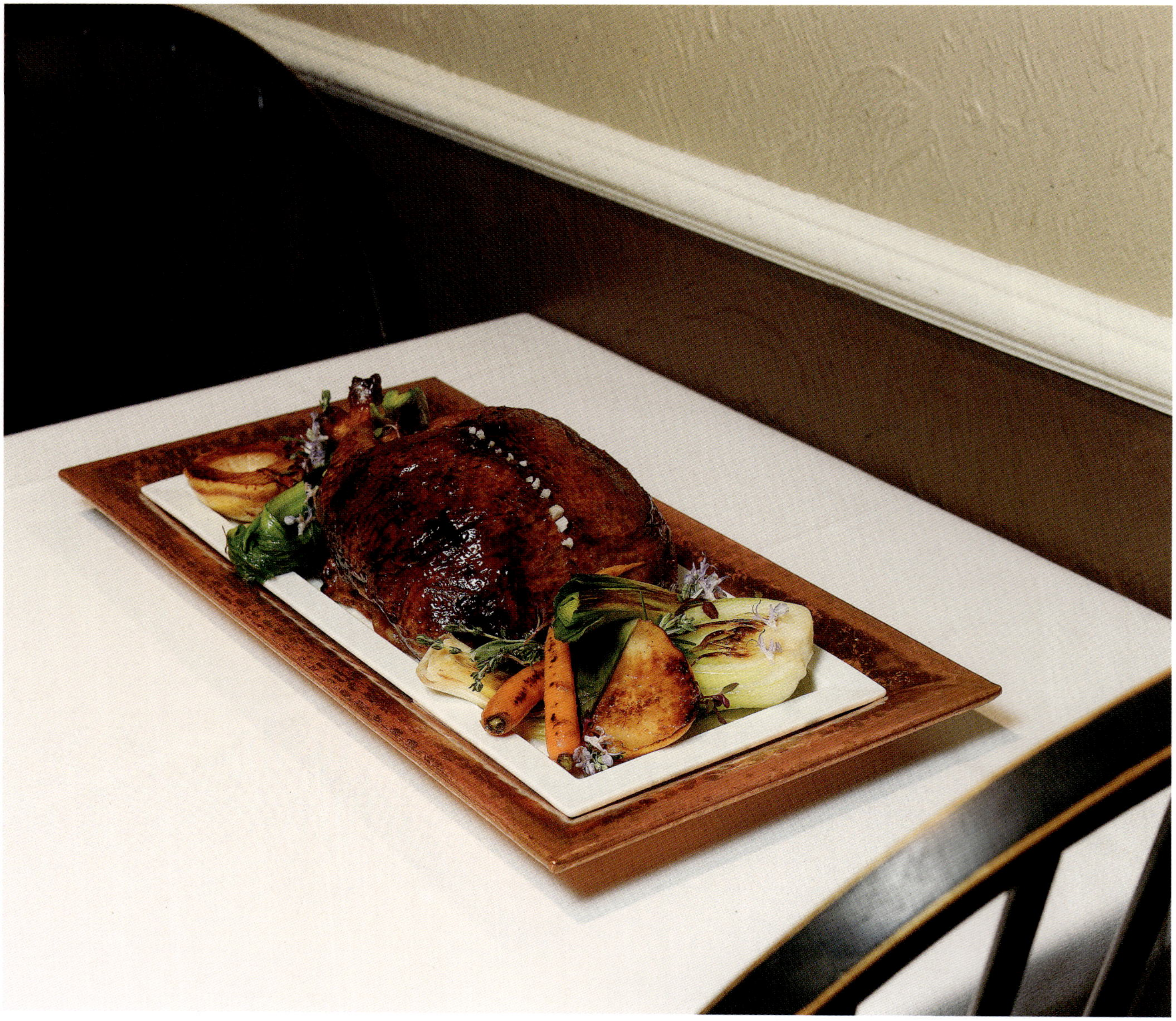

Whole Roasted Duck with Heirloom Apples

1 four-to-six-pound Long Island duck
salt and pepper
olive oil

3 cinnamon sticks
1 cup wild clover honey

4 heirloom apples, cored and cut into cubes
2 parsnips, peeled and cut in half
2 carrots, peeled and cut in half
4 shallots, peeled
1 large bay leaf
4 sprigs fresh thyme
4 tablespoons butter

Serves 2-4

Preheat oven to 375°. Season the duck, inside and out, with salt and pepper. Rub the skin with olive oil and place in oven for 1 hour and 40 minutes, basting every 15 minutes. Prior to serving, glaze the duck with cinnamon honey and roast for an additional 10 minutes. Remove from oven, transfer to a large serving tray, and arrange the roasted apples and vegetables around it.

Cinnamon Honey

Place the cinnamon sticks in a heavy saucepan and toast for 1 minute. Add the honey and let the mixture come to a simmer. Remove from heat and let steep for 1 hour.

Roasted Heirloom Apples and Fall Vegetables

In a large pan over medium-high heat, sauté the apples, carrots, parsnips, and shallots until they start to caramelize. Reduce the heat and add the bay leaf, thyme, and butter. Sauté for another minute and then place the vegetables in the oven with the duck to finish cooking until tender—about 25 minutes.

Grilled Tuna with Soy-Ginger Sauce

Tuna steak

Chantenay Carrot Purée

1 cup peeled and sliced ginger
Chantenay carrots
sesame oil
water

bok choy, blanched
Oaktree shiitake mushrooms, roasted
chickpeas, held in cooking liquid

Soy-Ginger Dressing

2 cups shallots, minced
1 cup ginger, minced
1 bottle sherry vinegar
1 small bottle oyster sauce, Panda label
½ cup soy sauce
canola oil, as needed

½ pound mirepoix

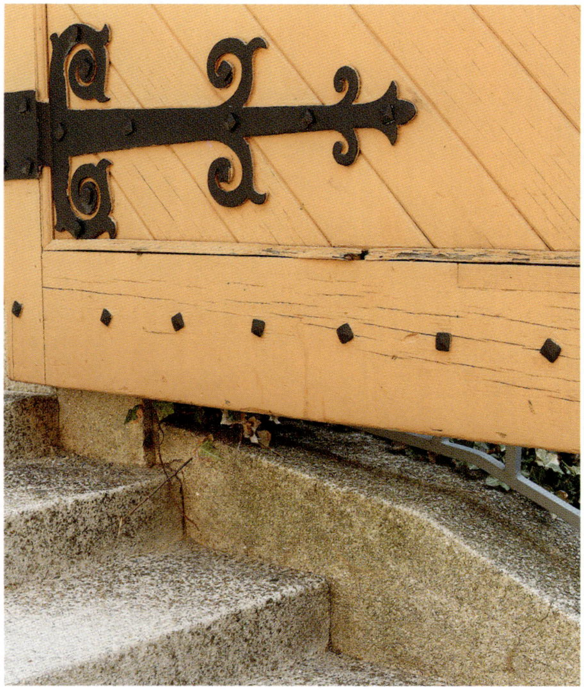

Served with Chantenay Carrot Purée, Oaktree Shiitake, Baby Bok Choy, and Chickpeas

The fish is grilled medium-rare, with steaks about ½ or ¾-inch thick, allowing the fish to cook quickly.

For the dressing mince the shallots and ginger extra-fine. Combine the first 5 ingredients in a bowl and cover with canola oil up to 1 inch above.

To make the purée, add 1 cup peeled and sliced ginger to the Chantenay carrots. Cover with water and a couple splashes of sesame oil. Bring to a boil and simmer until done. Purée and pass through a tamis. Hang to drain excess liquid.

Blanch baby bok choy in a lot of salted water. Shock in ice water.

Remove stems from mushrooms and toss in canola oil. Lay out on a sheet tray lined with parchment paper and season. Roast at 350° for 10 minutes.

Soak the chickpeas overnight. Cover by 3 inches with water and add ½ pound of mirepoix. Cook until the chickpeas have a soft, creamy texture and no bite. Season and cool in liquid.

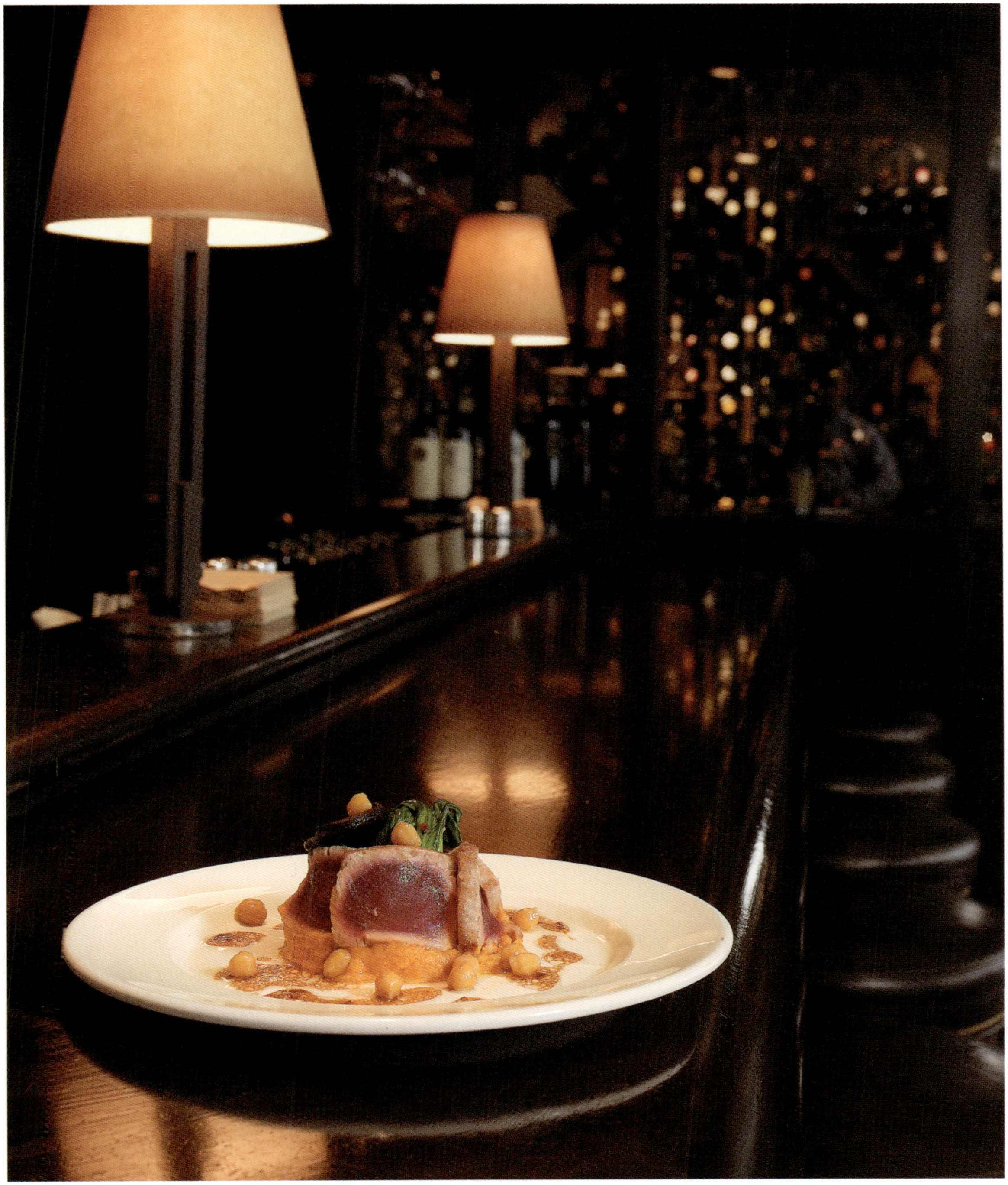

Harvest

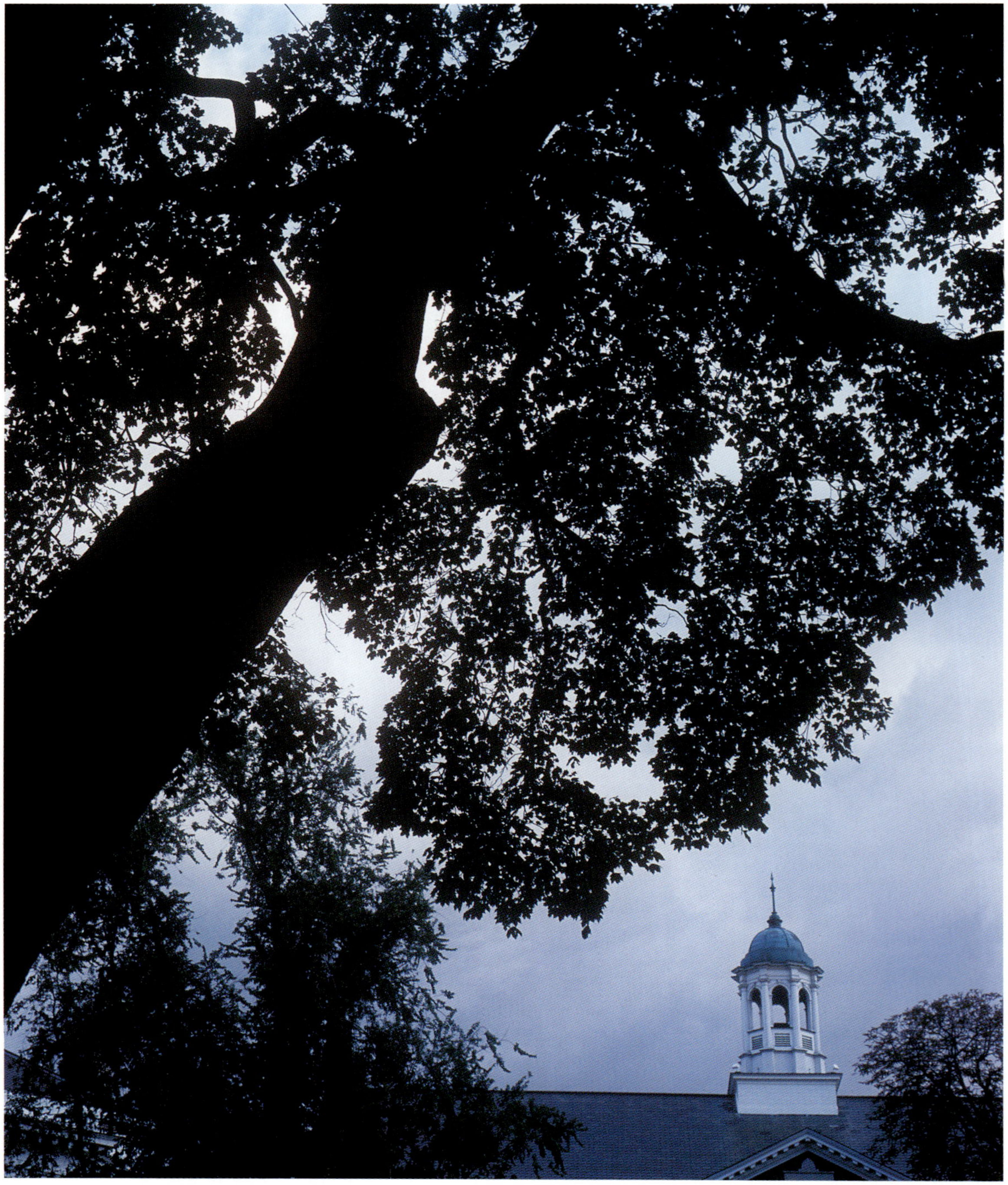

Mexican Vanilla Cheesecake with Pear-Cranberry Compote

Finale

Cheesecake

2½ teaspoons cornstarch
¾ cup sour cream
16 ounces cream cheese
4 eggs
1¼ cup confectioners' sugar, sifted
2 teaspoons Mexican vanilla extract

Pear-Cranberry Compote

⅔ cup fresh cranberries
⅔ cup pear, peeled and diced
¼ cup orange juice concentrate
1¾ cups granulated sugar
1 vanilla bean, cut in half
1 piece cinnamon stick
½ cup water
½ cup Gewurztraminer wine

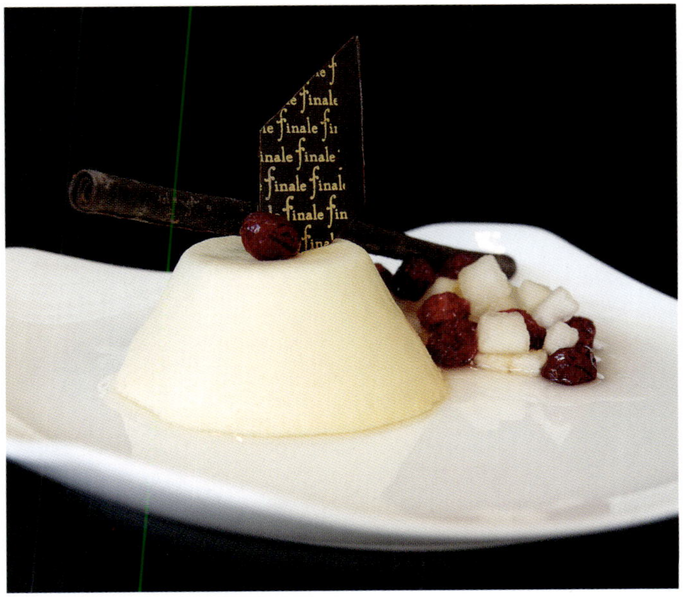

Cheesecake

Place cream cheese and sugar in a mixing bowl and cream on medium speed until creamy—scrape the sides of the bowl during mixing to prevent lumps. Mix approximately 5 minutes. In a separate bowl, crack eggs and add vanilla extract, then mix slightly to break up eggs. Slowly add eggs to the cream cheese-sugar mixture. Once the eggs are fully incorporated, stir in sour cream.

Preheat oven to 300°. Pour cheesecake into aluminum 4-ounce muffin cups. Place cups in an 8-x-13-inch pan. Pour boiling water into the pan until it reaches halfway up the cups. Bake until set, approximately 45-50 minutes. Allow to cool and then freeze for easy removal from the tins.

Pear-Cranberry Compote

Place cranberries in a wide saucepot. Then add all ingredients except the pears on top of the cranberries. Stirring occasionally, cook on a slow simmer until the cranberries start to become tender. While they're simmering, remove any froth that floats on top. Add the diced pears when the cranberries are slightly tender. Allow to simmer slightly longer to finish cooking the cranberries and to slightly cook the pears. Try to leave them still slightly firm. Serve over the cheesecakes.

chapter four

WINTER

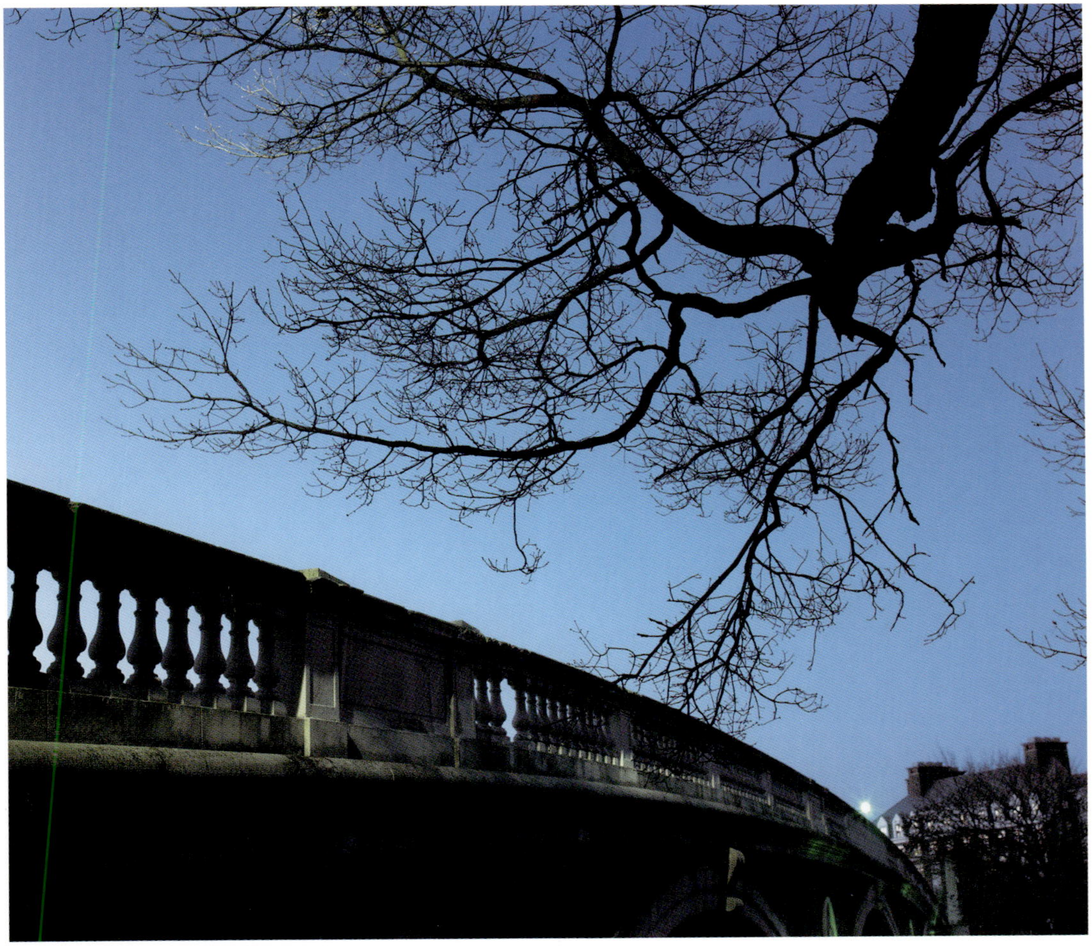

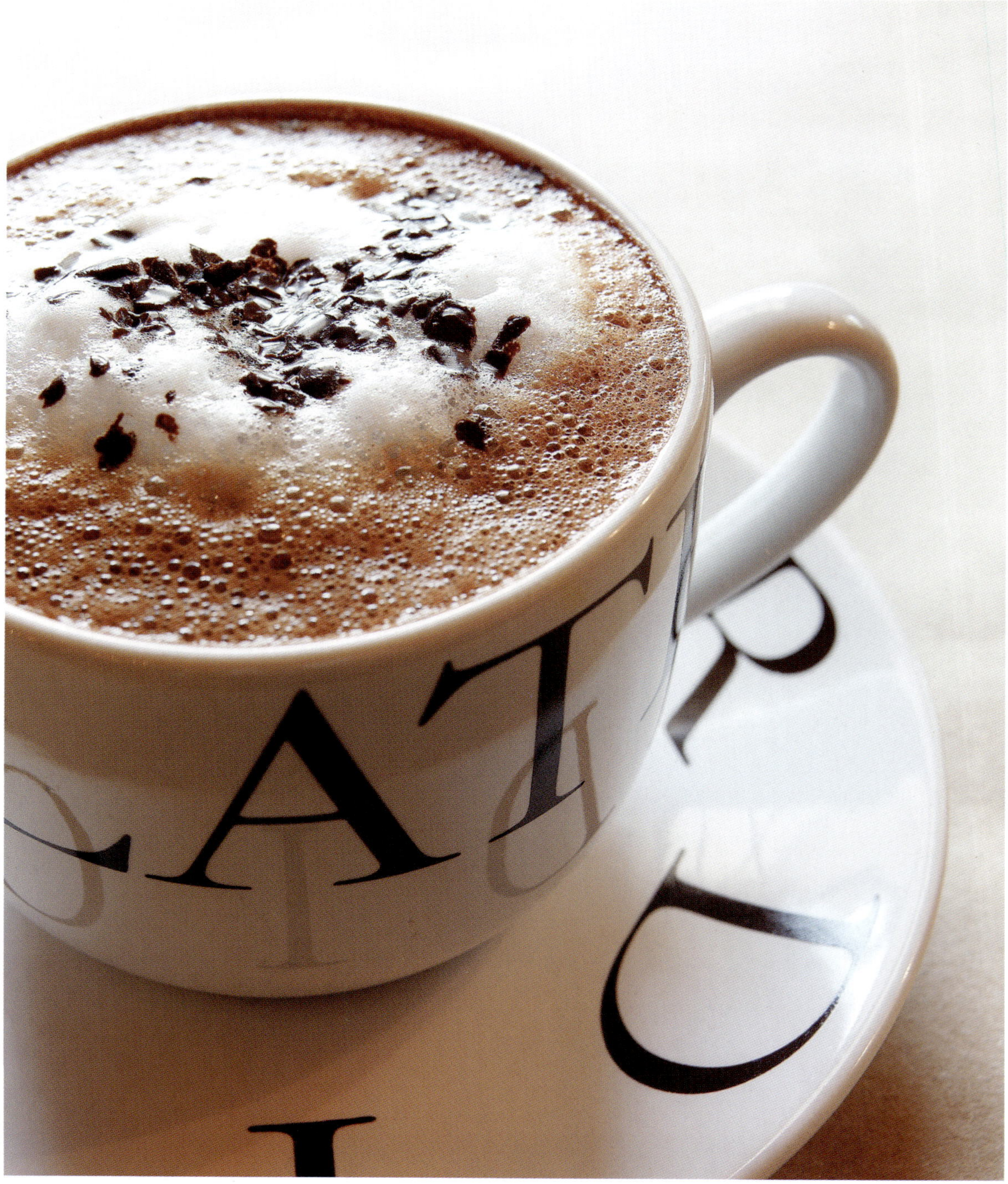

Burdick's Mocha

2 shots espresso
½ cup dark chocolate (68% cacao), shaved
1 cup 2% milk
1 teaspoon cocoa powder
chocolate shavings

Makes 12-ounce cup

Using a cappuccino machine, steam the milk to a frothing foam. Pour the steamed milk, holding back the foam, into a pitcher containing the shaved chocolate and cocoa powder. Whisk and reheat until hot. Pull the double shot of espresso into a cup or mug. Slowly add the hot chocolate so as not to disturb the crema. Garnish with a spoonful of milk foam and chocolate shavings.

Stovetop Method

Using a stovetop, whisk together the milk, shaved chocolate, and cocoa powder in a pan and heat until hot. Pour into a cup or mug over 2 ounces of very strong coffee or 2 shots of espresso. Garnish with whipped cream and chocolate shavings.

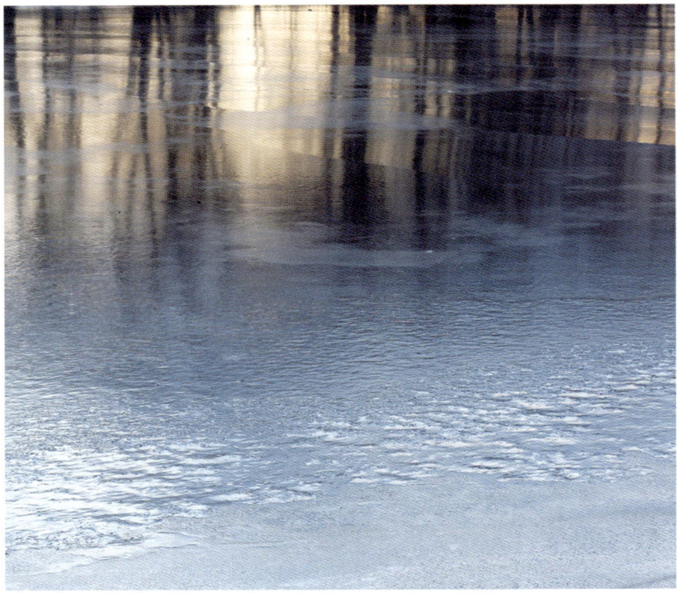

Grilled Steak de Provence with Lavender Aioli and Herb Salad

Steak

¼ cup whole fennel seeds, dry toasted in a skillet
4 cloves garlic
1 cup fresh basil leaves
1 cup fresh tarragon leaves
¼ cup fresh oregano leaves
2 tablespoons dried savory
1 tablespoon Dijon mustard
1 cup pure olive oil
4 ten-ounce flat iron steaks

Lavender Aioli

1 tablespoon dried edible lavender
1 tablespoon Dijon mustard
4 egg yolks
1 teaspoon minced garlic
1 teaspoon minced shallot
pinch sugar
1 teaspoon fresh lemon juice
1 cup canola oil
kosher salt
fresh ground black pepper

Herb Salad

1 ounce Banyuls vinegar (or substitute sherry vinegar)
1 ounce virgin olive oil
¼ cup fresh tarragon leaves
¼ cup fresh flat leaf parsley leaves
¼ cup fresh chervil leaves
¼ cup chives cut into 1 inch pieces
½ cup thin red radish slices
kosher salt
freshly ground black pepper

Pommes Frites

2-3 very large 40-count Idaho potatoes
canola oil for frying
kosher salt

In a food processor, purée the first 8 ingredients until smooth. Thoroughly coat the steaks with the marinade and marinate for 24 hours. Preheat grill until very hot. Season the steaks on both sides with freshly ground black pepper and kosher salt. Grill for 3-4 minutes per side for medium-rare. Let the steaks rest for 4 minutes before slicing against the grain. Serve with lavender aioli and herb salad.

Steep the dried lavender with 2 tablespoons hot tap water for 5 minutes. Add the lavender, Dijon, egg yolk, garlic, shallot, sugar, and lemon juice to the bowl of a small food processor. Purée until smooth, making sure to scrape the sides with a rubber spatula. With the machine running, slowly drizzle the canola oil in forming an emulsion. If the aioli gets too thick, a few drops of cold water can be added. Season well with kosher salt and freshly ground black pepper. The aioli is ready to serve, but will improve if left to rest in the refrigerator for a couple hours.

Mix the vinegar and oil together. Just before serving, toss all the herbs and radish together with the vinaigrette. Season with kosher salt and fresh ground black pepper.

Pommes Frites

The potatoes should be aged for 3-5 weeks at 50-60 degrees, in a dark area. The potatoes should be covered to prevent exposure to light, but still need to breathe, so don't seal them in an airtight container. The aging process will help reduce the natural sugar in the potato.

Wash the aged potatoes thoroughly. Slice them lengthwise on a French mandolin set as thick as it will go to create long shoe strings. Immediately submerge the potatoes in very hot tap water and allow them to sit for at least one hour.

Preheat canola oil to 325°. Blanch the frites in the oil until they become leathery, about 4 minutes. Drain on paper towels and store in the refrigerator until ready to serve.

To serve preheat canola oil to 350 degrees. Fry the frites until golden and crispy, about 2 minutes. Drain on paper towels and season well with salt. Serve immediately.

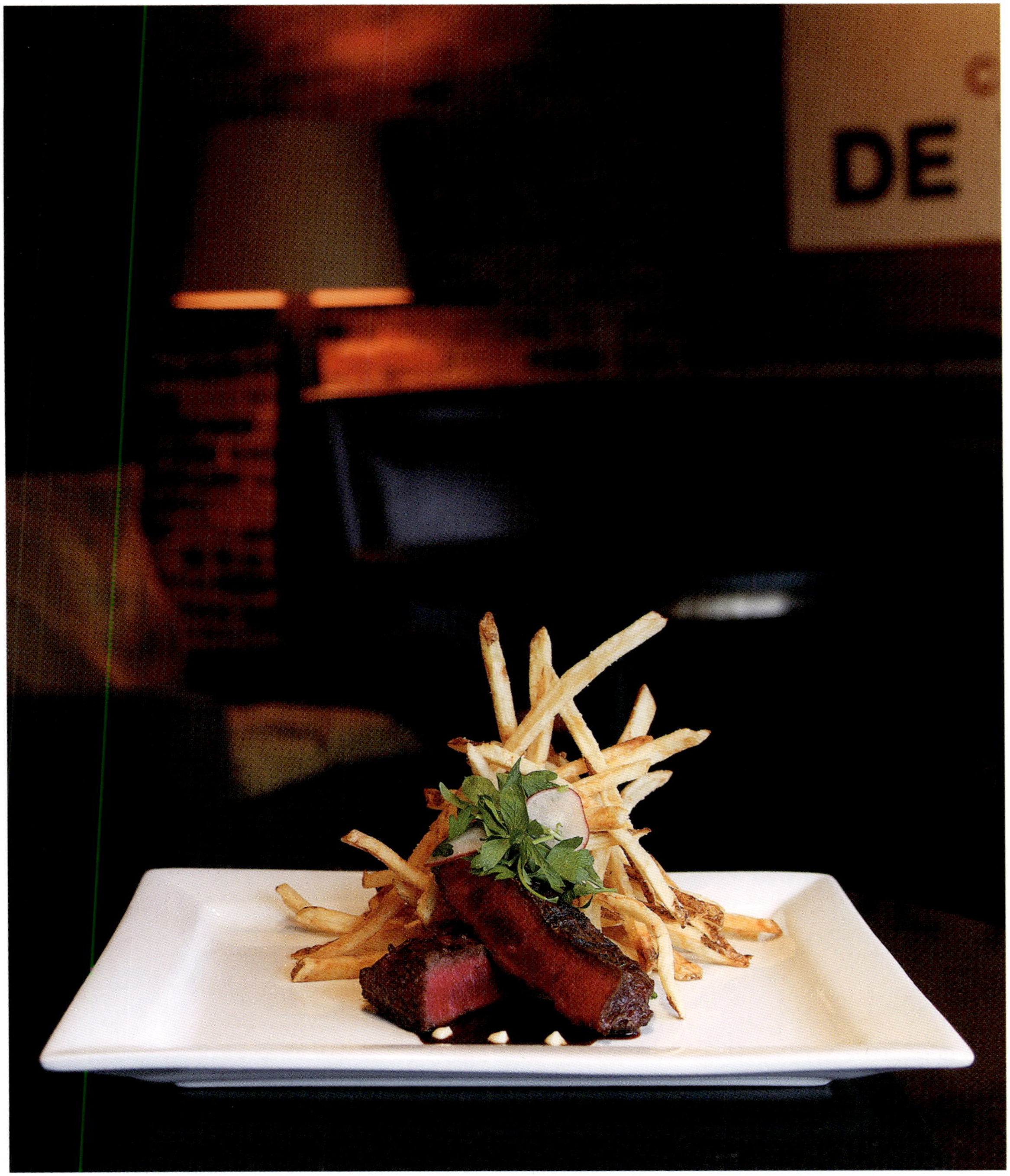
DE

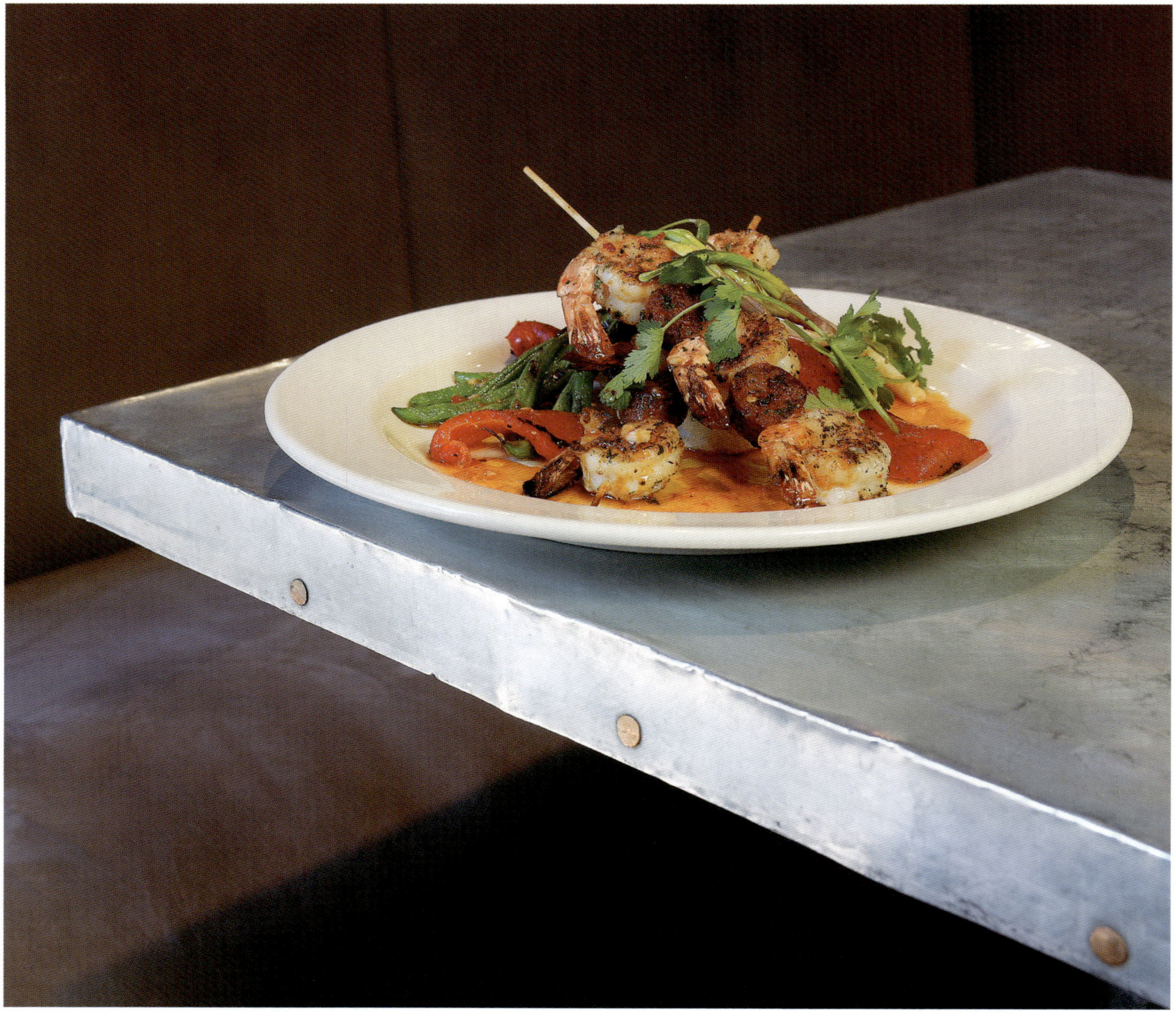

Shrimp with Chorizo, Yucca, and Ponzu Vinaigrette

Shrimp and Chorizo

1 pound shrimp, peeled and deveined
¼ Scotch Bonnet pepper
zest of ½ lemon
1 clove garlic
½ cup extra-virgin olive oil
½ teaspoon fennel seed
½ teaspoon coriander
1 half-pound chorizo sausage
8-inch wood skewers soaked in water (prevents burning on the grill)

Ponzu Vinaigrette

½ cup ponzu
1 cup lime juice
¼ cup rice wine vinegar
1 teaspoon sambal
1 clove garlic, minced
2 teaspoons fish sauce
1 teaspoon chili oil
½ teaspoon Sriracha

Crispy Yucca

3 medium yucca, peeled
canola oil for frying
1 teaspoon salt
pinch white pepper
milk and water

Additional Vegetables

12 scallions, cleaned and trimmed
6 Anaheim peppers

Garnish

6 branches cilantro, cleaned

Preheat oven to 350°. Trim the outer "bark" from the yucca. Cut into 1-inch cubes, trimming any "wood"-like veins. Place in a large saucepan and pour in ½ inch milk. Then add water to cover and season with salt and a pinch of white pepper. Bring to a simmer, stirring occasionally, and cook for approximately 45 minutes. If the liquid evaporates before the yucca is soft, add more. When soft, remove from heat and let cool. (If it seems soupy, strain it.) Form the cooled yucca into 4-inch-round cakes. To crisp the yucca, place a sauté pan over high heat with enough canola oil to cover the bottom. When the oil is hot, place the cakes in the pan and turn the flame down to medium. Let them fry until golden, then with a spatula carefully turn them over and place the pan in the oven. Bake until they're hot inside, approximately 10 minutes. Turn off the oven but leave the yucca cakes in to keep them warm until serving.

In a bowl, combine the Scotch Bonnet pepper, lemon zest, garlic, and olive oil, then blend or pass through a food processor. Crush the fennel seed and the coriander and mix them in with a spoon. Toss the shrimp in this mixture so that every piece gets covered and let marinate for at least 1 hour in the refrigerator.

Remove the chorizo from its casing and cut it into ½-inch rounds. Set aside. Once the shrimp have marinated, assemble the skewers, alternating shrimp with chorizo. Plan on 2 skewers per person. Set aside in the refrigerator until grill time.

For the vinaigrette, add the lime juice to a small saucepan and reduce it by half. Add the minced garlic to the warm reduced lime juice and let it cool. Once the juice has cooled, add the rest of the ingredients and salt to taste. Pour the vinaigrette into a container and store at room temperature. This vinaigrette will keep for several weeks.

Meanwhile, pull the shrimp and chorizo skewers from the refrigerator and grill over a medium-low fire for approximately 8 minutes. Toss the scallions and Anaheim peppers in olive oil and grill them until slightly charred.

Place the yucca cake in the center of a plate, with two skewers on top. Arrange the scallions and peppers. Pour some vinaigrette over the top of everything and garnish with cilantro.

Khar Saiko Kroeung (Braised Beef Short Ribs)

2 pounds Coleman beef short ribs
½ cup peeled ginger, thinly sliced

Paste

dried New Mexico chilis, soaked, seeded, and deveined
garlic cloves, coarsely chopped
½ cup water
5 tablespoons vegetable oil
3 tablespoons sugar
2 tablespoons fish sauce
1 tablespoon mushroom soy sauce
1 teaspoon salt
1 teaspoon black pepper
1 cup chicken broth
1 cup green coconut juice
¼ cup tamarind juice

Garnish

cilantro sprigs
cucumber slices

Put the beef in a bowl. Grind the ginger slices with a mortar and pestle, adding them a few at a time until you've extracted most of the juice, or use a mini-chop to make a wet paste. Squeeze the juice from the fibers—you should have 1½ to 2 tablespoons—and stir into the beef; discard the ginger solids. Let the beef marinate for at least 10 minutes.

While the beef marinates, make the paste. Blend all the ingredients in a blender until smooth, 2 to 3 minutes.

Heat the oil in a large pot over medium-high heat. Add the paste and cook, stirring occasionally, until the liquid is reduced by half, about 40 minutes.

Add the coconut and tamarind juices and cook for another 20 minutes. If the sauce is too thin at this point, increase the heat and reduce further; the sauce should be fairly thick.

Cook the beef to desired doneness. Garnish with cilantro sprigs and serve with cucumber slices and rice.

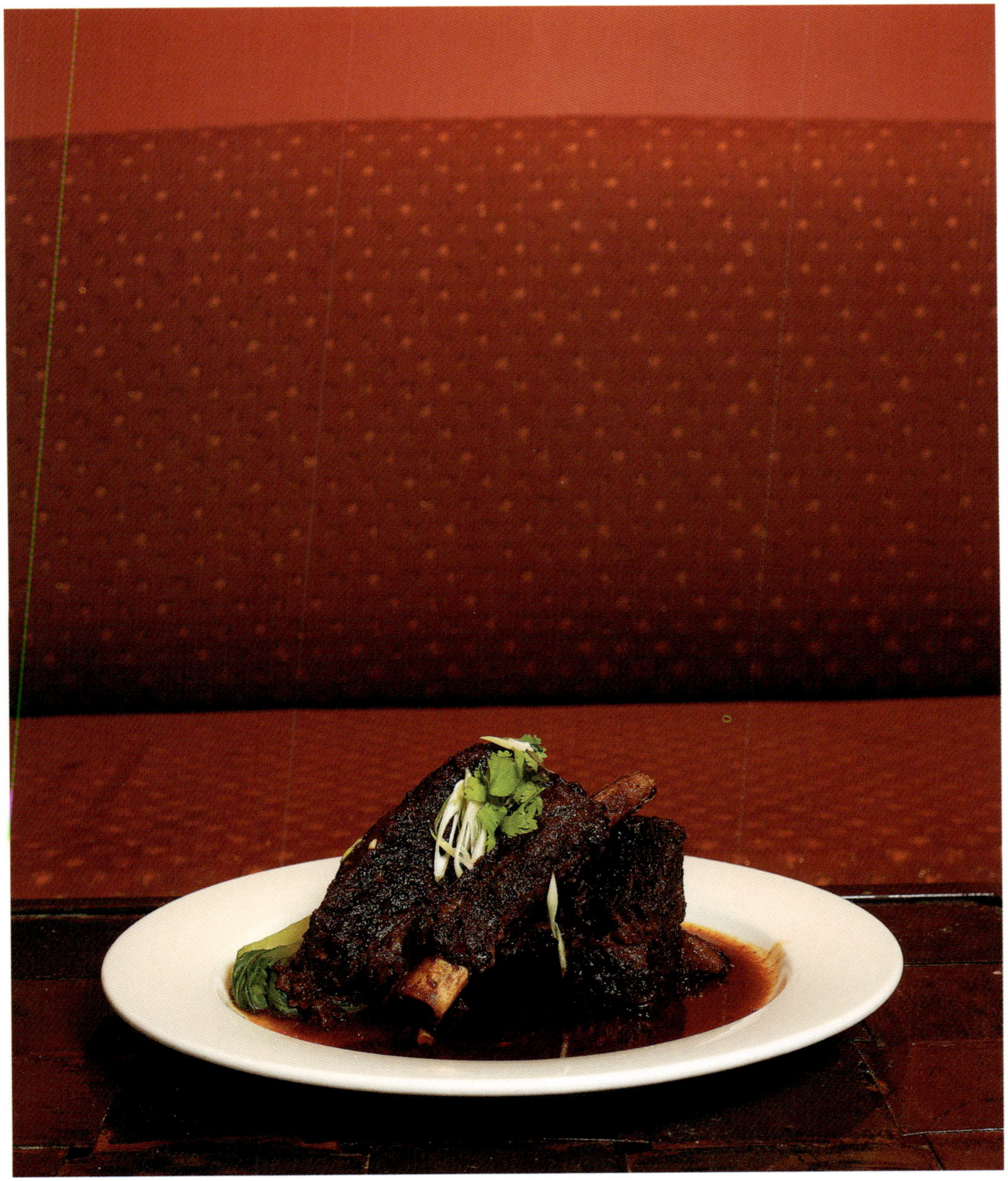

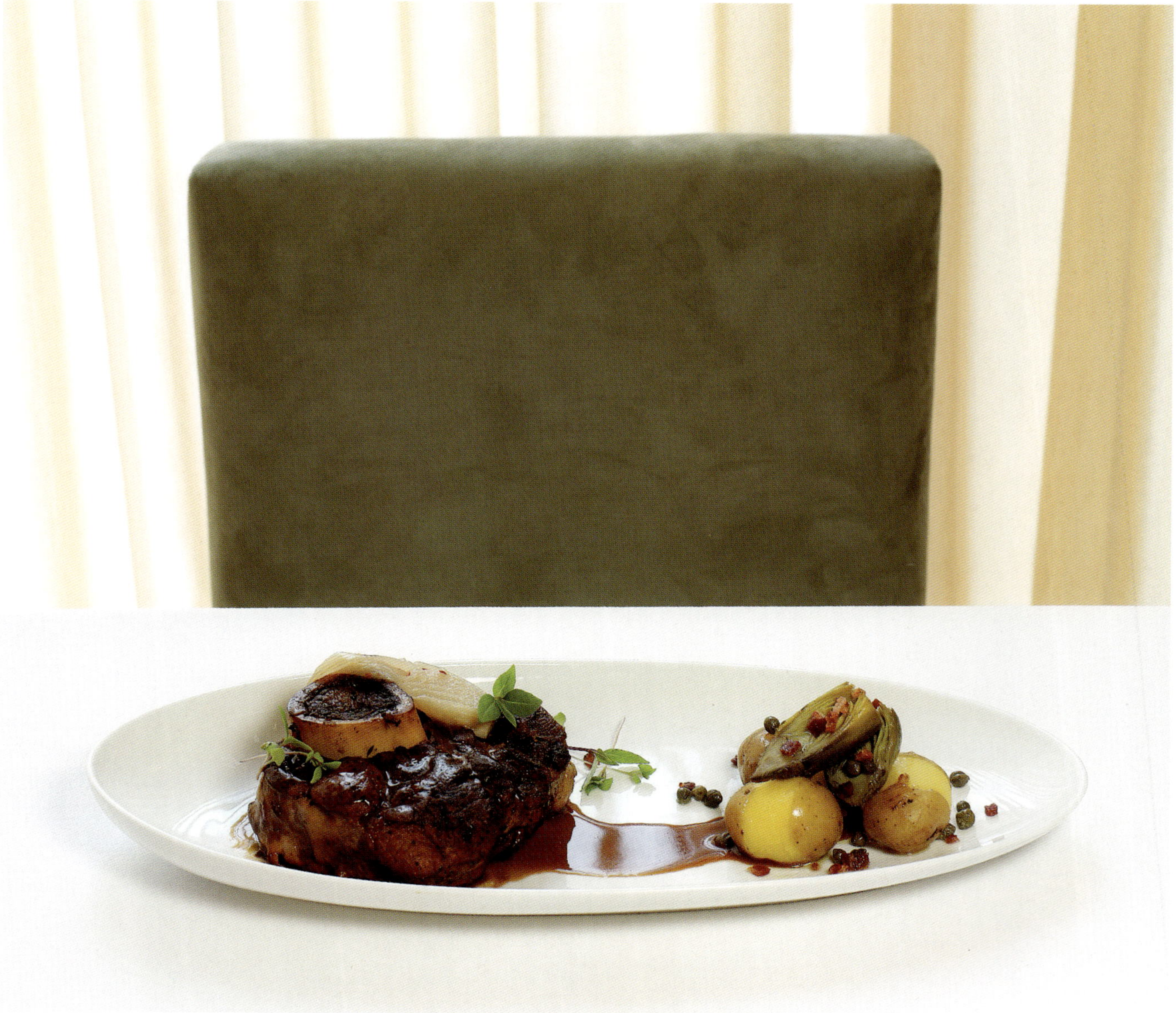

Braised Veal Shank with Marsala

4 large, meaty veal shanks, about 2 inches thick
kosher salt and freshly ground black pepper
3 tablespoons vegetable oil
3 ounces diced pancetta
1 onion, cut into 1-inch dice
1 stalk celery, peeled and cut into 1-inch dice
1 carrot, peeled and cut into 1-inch dice
4 cloves garlic, smashed and peeled
2 bay leaves
1 cup chopped tomatoes, fresh or canned
zest of ½ lemon, in thick strips
zest of ¼ orange, in thick strips
¾ cup white wine
¾ cup Marsala
1 quart chicken stock
1 tablespoon chopped fresh thyme
2 tablespoons unsalted butter
6 baby artichokes, cooked and halved
8 small red bliss potatoes, cooked
1 tablespoon lemon juice
4 tablespoons chopped fresh parsley

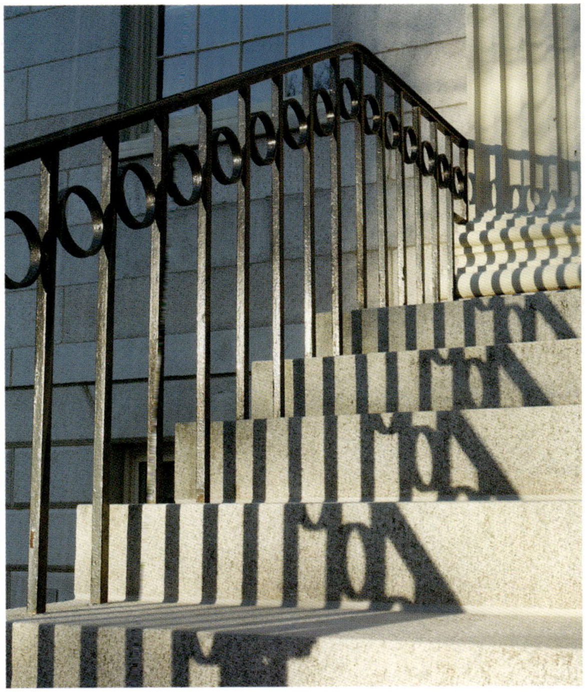

Preheat oven to 325°.

Season the veal shanks all over with salt and pepper. Heat the vegetable oil in a large braising pan or Dutch oven over medium-high heat. Sear the shanks on both sides until brown. Transfer the shanks to a platter. Lower the heat to medium. Add the pancetta, onion, celery, carrot, and garlic and season with salt and pepper. Sauté, stirring occasionally, until the vegetables begin to brown, about 7 minutes.

Add the bay leaves, tomato, and zests and cook for 3 minutes. Add the wine and Marsala, bring to a boil, then lower the heat to a simmer and reduce by ¾. Add stock and reduce again by ½. Return the shanks to the pan. The liquid should come ⅓ up the sides of the veal. Reduce the liquid a bit more if necessary. Cover with a piece of parchment, then cover that with a lid, and braise in the oven for 3 hours. The meat should be tender enough to cut with a spoon.

Remove the shanks from the braising juices and keep warm. Strain the juices into a clean pan and reduce until they will coat the back of a spoon. Add the thyme and return the shanks to the pan.

Heat the butter in a small sauté pan over medium heat. Add the artichokes and potatoes, season with salt and pepper, and toss until heated through. Add the lemon juice and parsley and toss well.

To serve, put the veal shanks in the center of 4 warm plates, arrange the artichokes and potatoes around the veal, pour the juices over the veal, and serve with a small spoon for the marrow.

Roast Chicken with Lime and Achiote

2 three-pound chickens, giblets removed

Marinade

2 tablespoons achiote powder
2 tablespoons ground cumin
10 garlic cloves, smashed
juice of 2 limes
1 tablespoon dried oregano
3 scallions, chopped
1 teaspoon pepper
¼ cup olive oil
1 heaping tablespoon chopped fresh mint leaves

2 tablespoons unsalted butter
3 garlic cloves, minced
juice of 1 lime

1 teaspoon kosher salt
½ teaspoon black pepper
1½ cups hot water
juice of 1 lime

Serves 6

To marinate the chicken, place in a shallow dish. Place all marinade ingredients in a medium bowl and mix to combine. Pour the marinade over the chicken, taking care to coat the chicken evenly on all sides—including the inside. Cover and refrigerate at least 24 and up to 48 hours, basting the chicken with the marinade every 8 hours.

Preheat the oven to 500°.

To make the baste, place the butter, garlic and lime juice in a small pot over low heat. Cook until the butter is just melted, 1-2 minutes.

Pour off excess marinade and season chicken with the salt and pepper. Place chicken in a shallow roasting pan and place in the oven. After 30 minutes, reduce oven temperature to 350° and baste chicken with ⅓ basting liquid. Continue cooking, basting every 20 minutes, until the leg twists loosely and the juices from the thigh run clear, or until a meat thermometer inserted in the deepest part of the thigh—but not touching the bone—reaches 165°, about 1 hour. Remove chicken from pan and set aside to rest.

Pour off all but 2 tablespoons of the oil and place the roasting pan over medium heat—you may need to use two burners. Add 1½ cups hot water or chicken stock. Bring to a boil, stirring gently to remove any browned bits still stuck to the bottom of the pan. Continue boiling until slightly reduced, 2-3 minutes. Off heat, add lime juice.

Cut the chicken into serving pieces and divide among 6 plates. Strain the sauce over the chicken, distributing evenly. Garnish with watercress.

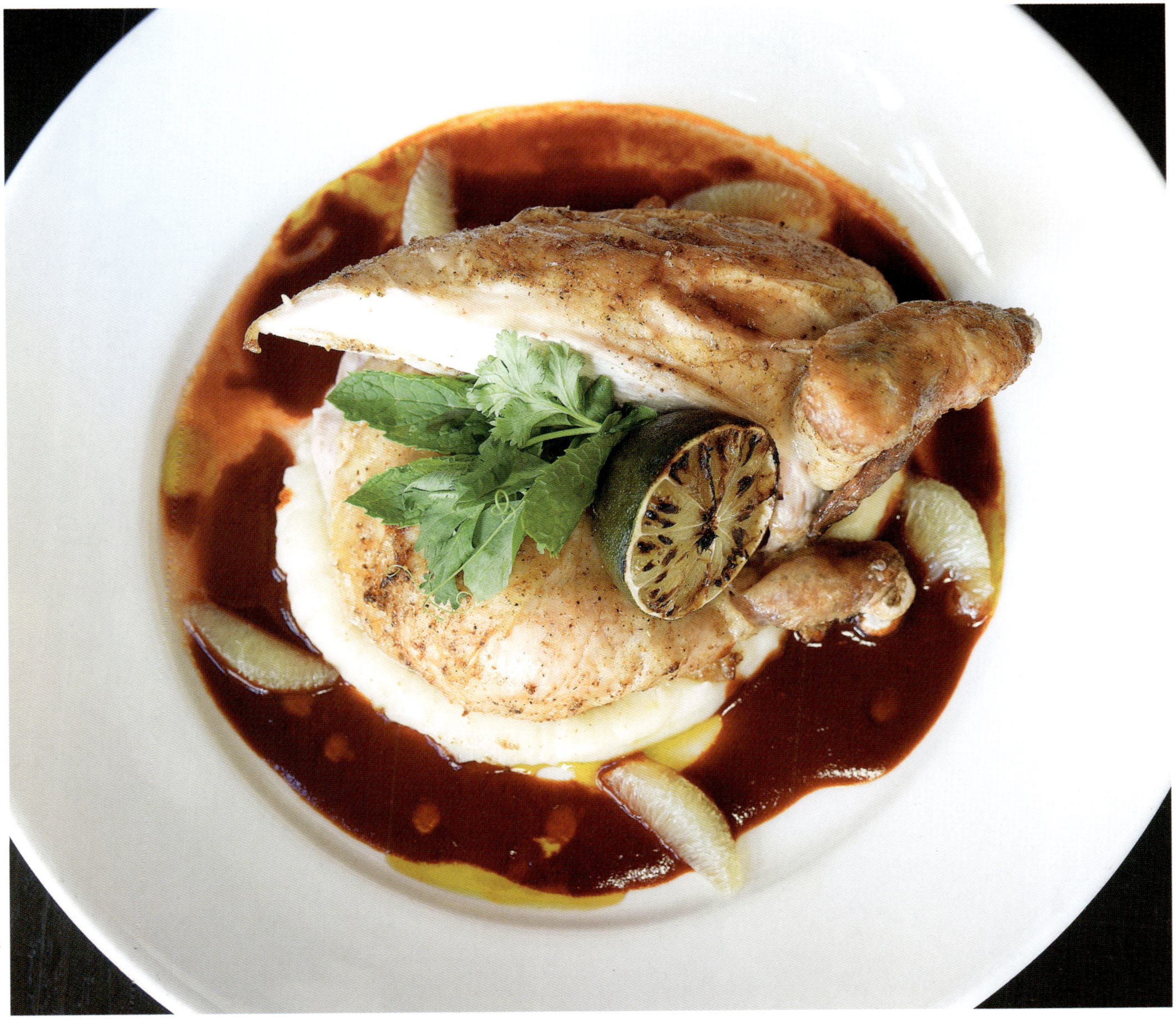

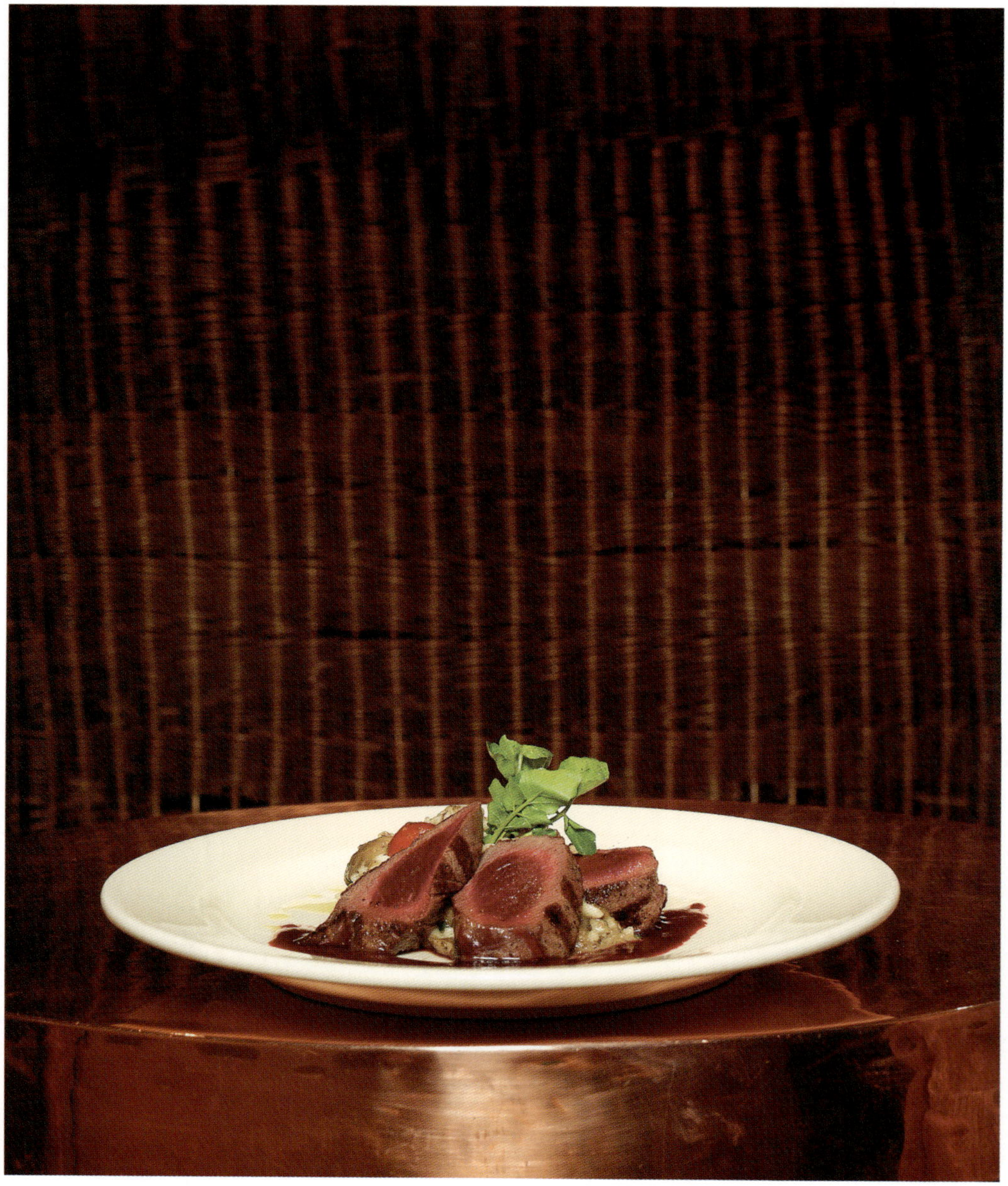

Grilled Venison with Mushroom Risotto

Casablanca

24 ounces venison, Denver leg
truffle oil

Mushroom Risotto

1 cup arborio rice
½ cup white wine
½ white onion, diced
2 cups chicken stock
½ pound oyster mushrooms, roasted with olive oil, salt, and pepper
1 lemon, juiced
2 tablespoons chopped parsley
2 tablespoons Parmesan cheese
½ pint cherry tomatoes, halved
2 tablespoons butter

Cranberry Sauce

2 cups ruby port
1 cup fresh cranberries
½ cup sugar

Serves 4

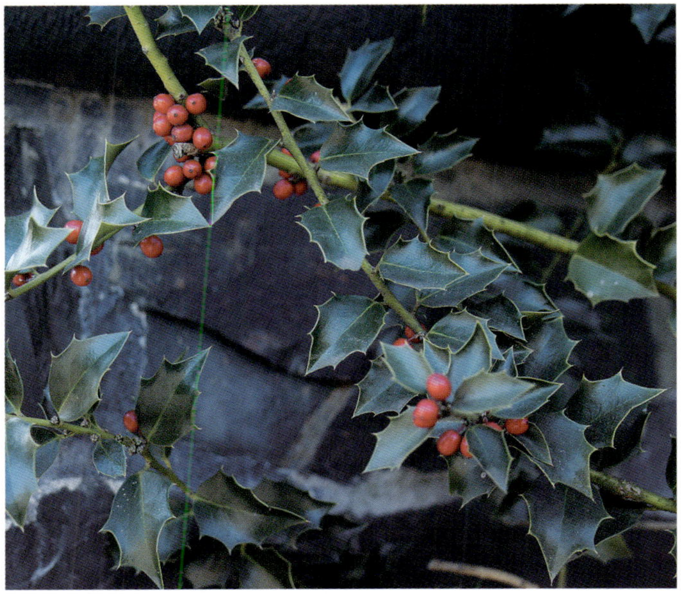

Mushroom Risotto

In a large pan, sauté the onion in olive oil until tender. Add the arborio rice and toast slightly in the hot oil. Add the white wine and reduce until most of the liquid is gone. Add the chicken stock and water, if needed, to cover. Cook until the rice is nearly done. Add the rest of the ingredients and season with salt and pepper.

Cranberry Sauce

Simmer the cranberries in the port and sugar until the liquid is reduced by half. Purée and strain.

Grilled Venison

Season the venison with salt and pepper and rub with oil. Grill to the desired doneness. Let the meat rest and slice. Serve with the risotto and cranberry sauce and drizzle with truffle oil.

Loin of Farm Pork with Cauliflower and Young Potatoes

4 well-cleaned 6-ounce pieces of pork loin
string for tying

20 very small potatoes
butter, browned
salt

1 head cauliflower
champagne vinegar
olive oil
1 quart milk
fresh whole nutmeg
salt and pepper

2 pounds pork bones or trim
1 small onion, sliced fine
1 rib celery, sliced fine
1 carrot, sliced fine
vegetable oil
butter

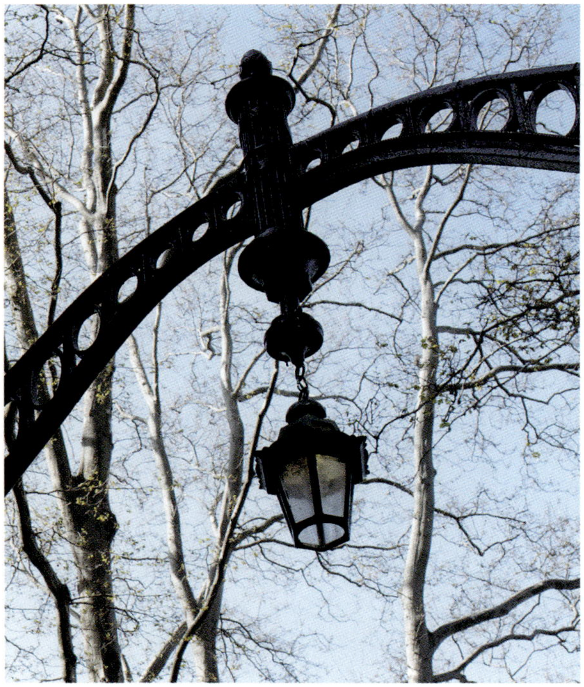

Sauce

Prepare a jus from the pork bones by searing them in a heavy pan. Caramelize them well and add the carrot, onion, and celery. Add a knob of butter and continue to brown the bones for 5 minutes. Strain off the grease and cover with water. Cook for 2 hours, then pass and reduce to a glaze. Place in a small saucepan, season, and finish with butter until shiny.

Potatoes

Cook very small potatoes in one layer in boiling water. Remove, slice in half, and finish in brown butter with salt.

Cauliflower

Trim some small "fleurettes" off the top of the head and blanch these in salted water. Remove from water and soak in 2 tablespoons vinegar and 2 tablespoons olive oil. Season. Cut the remaining cauliflower into chunks and cover with milk. Season with salt and pepper and a grating of nutmeg. Cook through and purée in the blender using the milk to dilute to the desired consistency. Keep hot.

Tie the loin pieces to create a uniform circle. Sear in oil, roast on all sides, and baste in butter. Let rest, remove string, and slice for the plate.

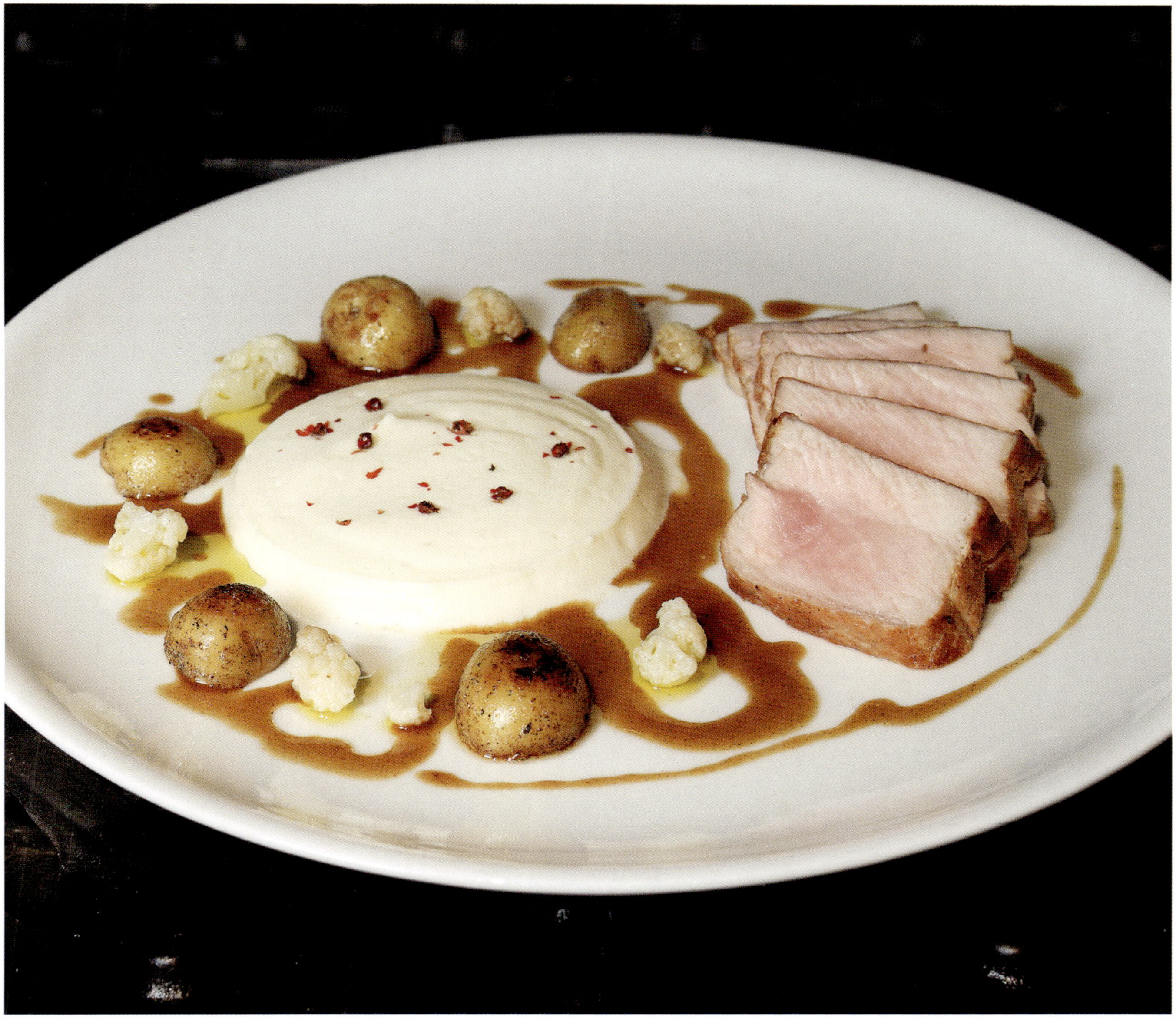

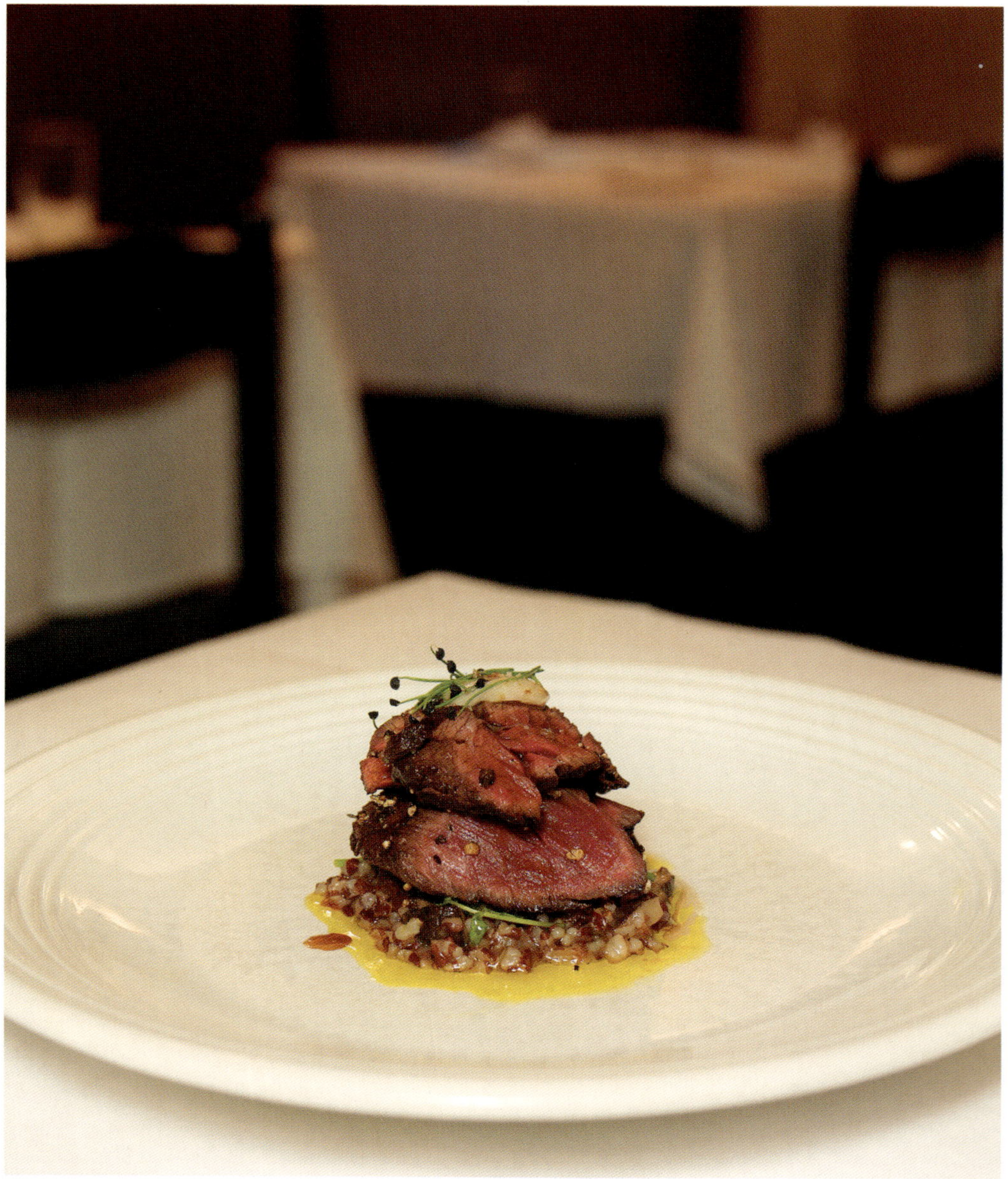

Red Chili-Marinated Skirt Steak

5 pounds skirt or hangar steak

Marinade

6 New Mexican dried red chilis, rehydrated
6 garlic cloves
1 tablespoon coriander seeds
1 tablespoon cumin seeds
2 cloves
10 allspice berries
1 tablespoon ground ginger
1 tablespoon dried thyme
2 teaspoons black peppercorns
1 cup canola oil
½ cup soy sauce
salt to taste

Grind all of the spices and seed the chilis. Put all marinade ingredients into a blender and purée. Rub on skirt steak and let sit overnight. Grill to desired level of doneness.

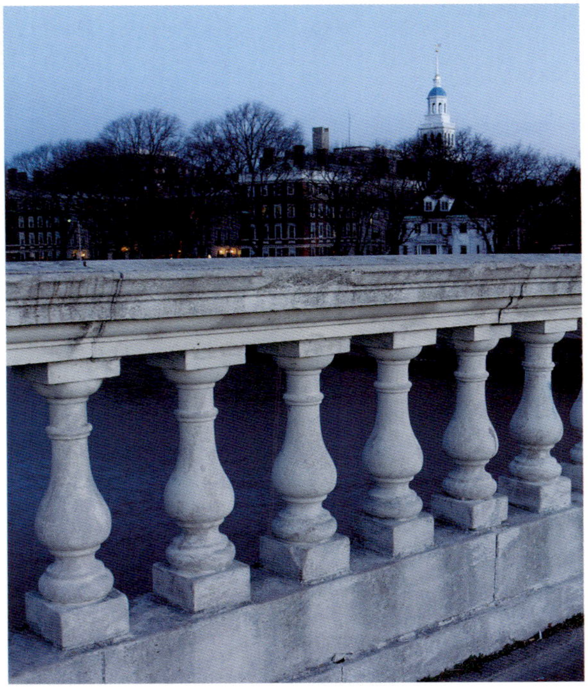

Craigie Street Bistrot

Alsatian Choucroute

1 large onion, julienne
4 ounces duck fat
1 teaspoon chopped garlic
4 bay leaves
1 ounce juniper berries
½ bunch fresh thyme
1 750ml bottle Riesling wine
6 pounds raw sauerkraut
1 pound slab smoked bacon
8 pieces ham shanks, cured and salted
1 quart chicken stock
8 large red bliss potatoes
4 pieces weisswurst (veal and chicken sausage)
4 pieces bauernwurst (salted smoked pork sausage)
8 pieces wiener (Vienna sausage)
8 pieces smoked pork chop, cooked

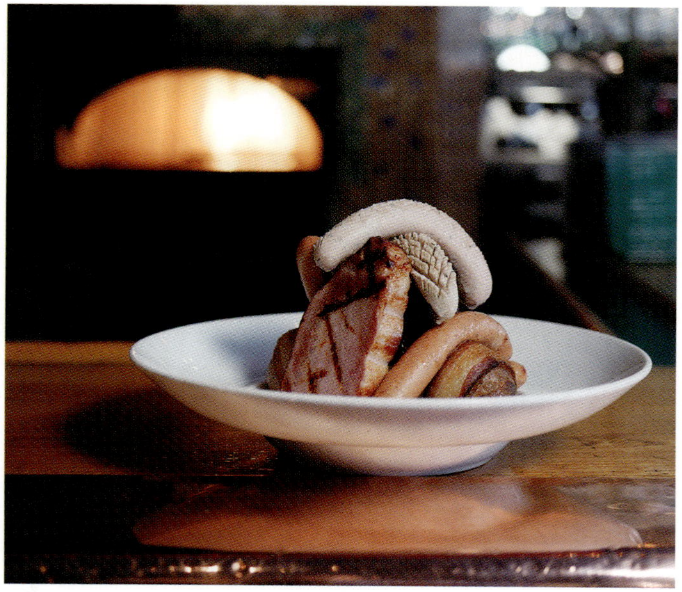

Wash the sauerkraut thoroughly and put aside. In a rondeau, melt the duck fat and sauté the onion until tender; add garlic, bay leaves, juniper berries, and thyme. Sear until golden-brown and deglaze with Riesling wine. Add half of the sauerkraut, place bacon and ham shanks in the middle, and then top with the remaining sauerkraut. Pour chicken stock over it, making sure it covers the sauerkraut—if there's not enough, add water. Cover the pan with foil and place in the oven at 350° for 1½ hours.

Wash the potatoes and steam them whole for 30-40 minutes, until tender. Peel them and set them aside.

Cut the sausages in half and warm them in boiling water. Take the sauerkraut out of the oven and remove the bacon and ham shanks. Slice the bacon in half. Place the sauerkraut in the center of a large oval tray, arrange the wursts, wiener, and warm potatoes around it, and place the bacon and pork shanks on top. Serve Dijon mustard on the side. Accompany with a glass of Riesling wine or beer.

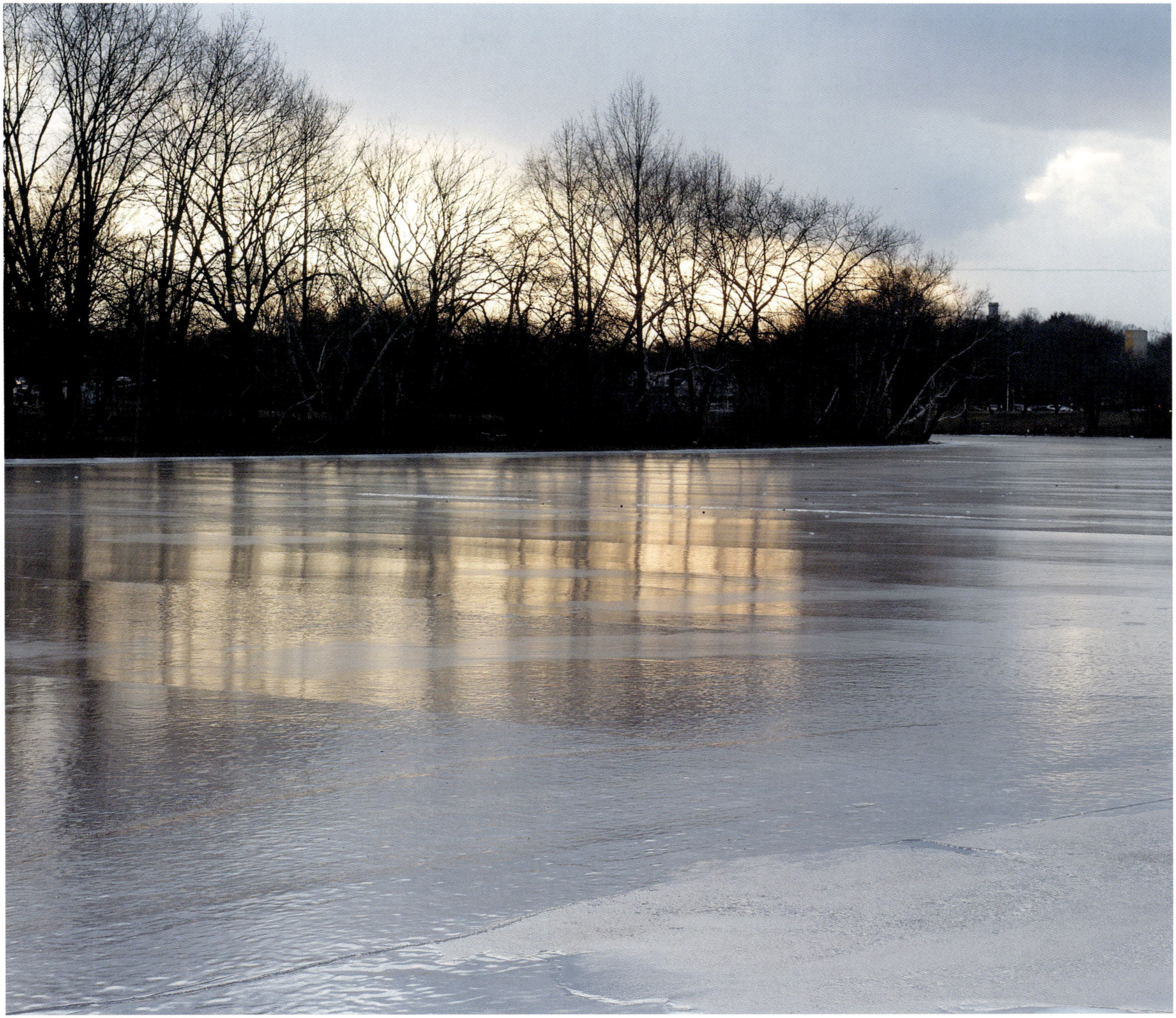

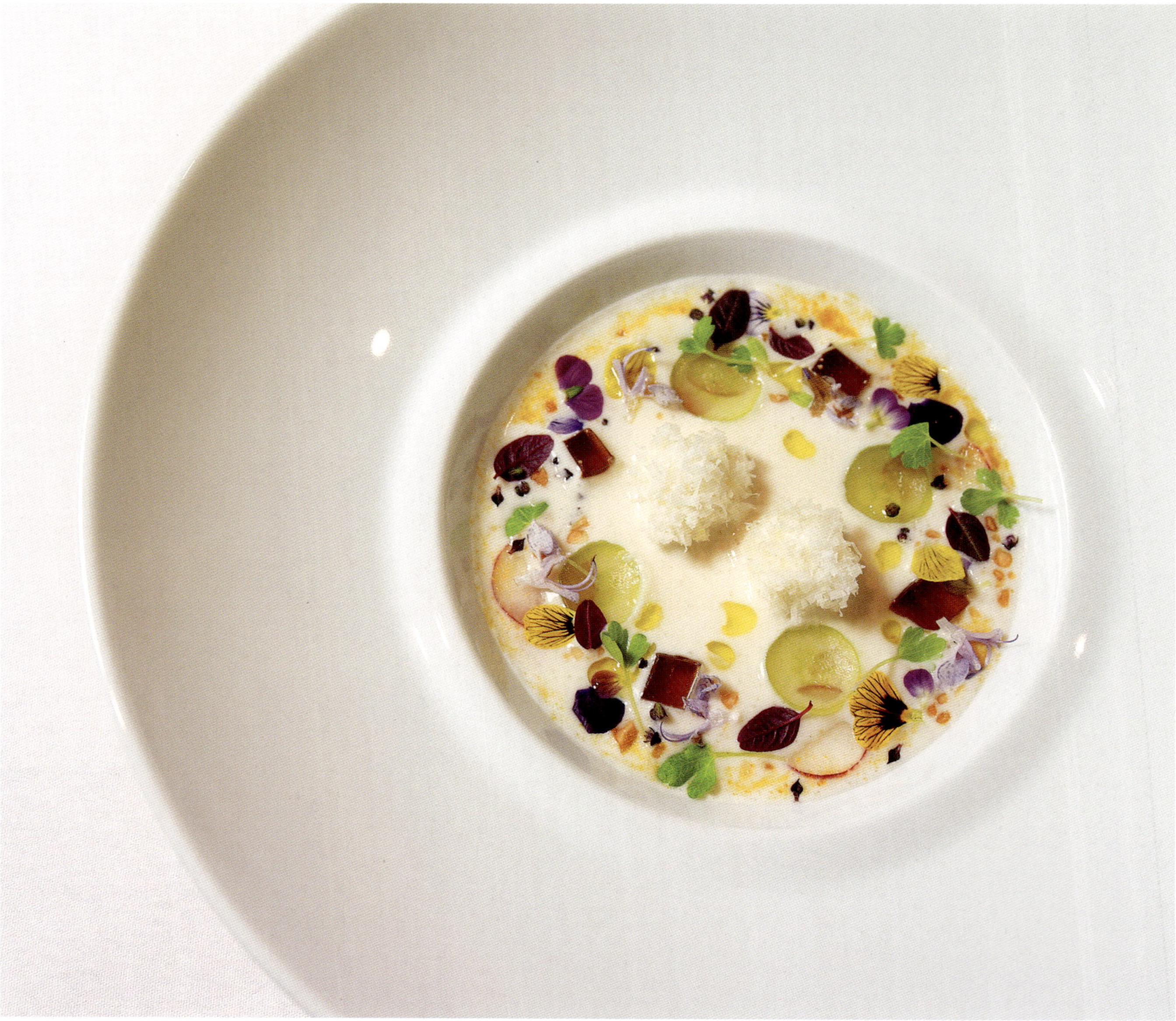

Coconut Tapioca with Tropical Fruit and Thai Basil

3 cups whole milk
¼ cup sugar
¼ cup tapioca
1 can coconut milk

1 ripe golden pineapple
1 fresh passion fruit
1 ripe mango
1 ripe papaya
simple syrup
Thai basil sprouts

Serves 4-6

For the Tapioca

In a heavy saucepan, combine the milk and sugar and bring to a boil. Be careful not to let this mixture boil over—it will scorch. Lower the heat to a medium-high flame and whisk in the tapioca to keep it from sticking to the bottom of the pot. When the tapioca is done, remove from heat, stir in the coconut milk, and season with a pinch of salt. Let chill for 1 hour before serving.

For the Fruit

With a small melon baller, cut out ¼-inch balls of fruit and place them in a mixing bowl, saving the seeds from the passion fruit. Add 2 tablespoons of simple syrup and the basil sprouts. Let sit at room temperature for 10 minutes before serving. If Thai basil sprouts aren't available, you can substitute thinly sliced Thai basil leaves.

To serve, spoon the tapioca into a serving dish and top with the marinated fruit and fresh passion fruit seeds.

Note

At the restaurant, we serve this dish as a composed dessert with toasted coconut parsnip cake and coconut sorbet.

Pomegranate-Lacquered Duck Breast

2 fresh ducklings, preferably with head and feet on

Sauce

Trimmings and bones of both ducklings
1 onion, diced small
1 rib celery, diced small
1 carrot, peeled and diced small
1 bay leaf
1 cup dry white wine
½ cup white port
2 quarts chicken stock
1 quart water
1 tablespoon butter
2 sprigs fresh thyme
2 sprigs fresh rosemary
½ black winter truffle, about the size of a golf ball, diced small

Potatoes

2 pounds Yukon Gold potatoes, peeled and sliced 1-inch thick
1 cup kosher salt
2 cups heavy cream
½ pound butter, cubed
1 tablespoon mace, freshly ground

Lacquer

½ cup pomegranate molasses
4 tablespoons olive oil
2 tablespoons sugar
1 teaspoon salt

Finish

Baby bok choy, blanched in salted water and drained well (serving size depends upon size of vegetable)
Sliced black truffle
Pomegranate seeds

Served with Spiced Potatoes and Black Truffle Jus

Have your butcher quarter the birds, saving all bones and trimmings. Reserve the legs and thighs for another meal; they'll keep in the freezer for up to 6 months. They can be substituted for the breast in the dish, but they require a bit more cooking, as legs and thighs should not be eaten medium-rare.

Sauce

Roast the bones in a 500° oven until golden brown. While they're roasting, put a pot large enough to hold all of the bones on the stove on medium heat. Melt the butter and add the carrot, onion, celery, and bay leaf. Sweat these vegetables, taking care not to brown them, about 10 minutes. Add white wine and port and reduce by half. Add the bones, chicken stock, and water. Bring to a boil, then reduce to a simmer for 1½ hours. Skim off any impurities that rise to the top and discard. Strain carefully through cheesecloth, then reduce on medium heat until viscous—by at least ¾. When the sauce seems to be thick enough, add the herbs and turn the heat off. Strain again after 10 minutes. Add the truffle just before serving. Season with salt.

Potatoes

Simmer the potatoes and salt together in enough water that it tastes like seawater, no saltier. When the potatoes are tender, pass through a food mill or a ricer. Heat up the cream and encorporate with a rubber spatula. Add the butter next, stirring gently but continuously. Season with the mace and salt.

Duck Breast and Lacquer

Season the duck breast liberally with salt and pepper and render skin-side down in a pan on medium heat until golden and crispy. You may need to pour off fat once or twice during this process. Flip the duck over and cook until medium-rare or medium, depending on the desired doneness. Let the duck rest on a plate for 4 minutes, skin-side up. Whisk lacquer ingredients together and paint a thick layer on the skin. Broil for 20 seconds or until the lacquer bubbles. Slice and serve.

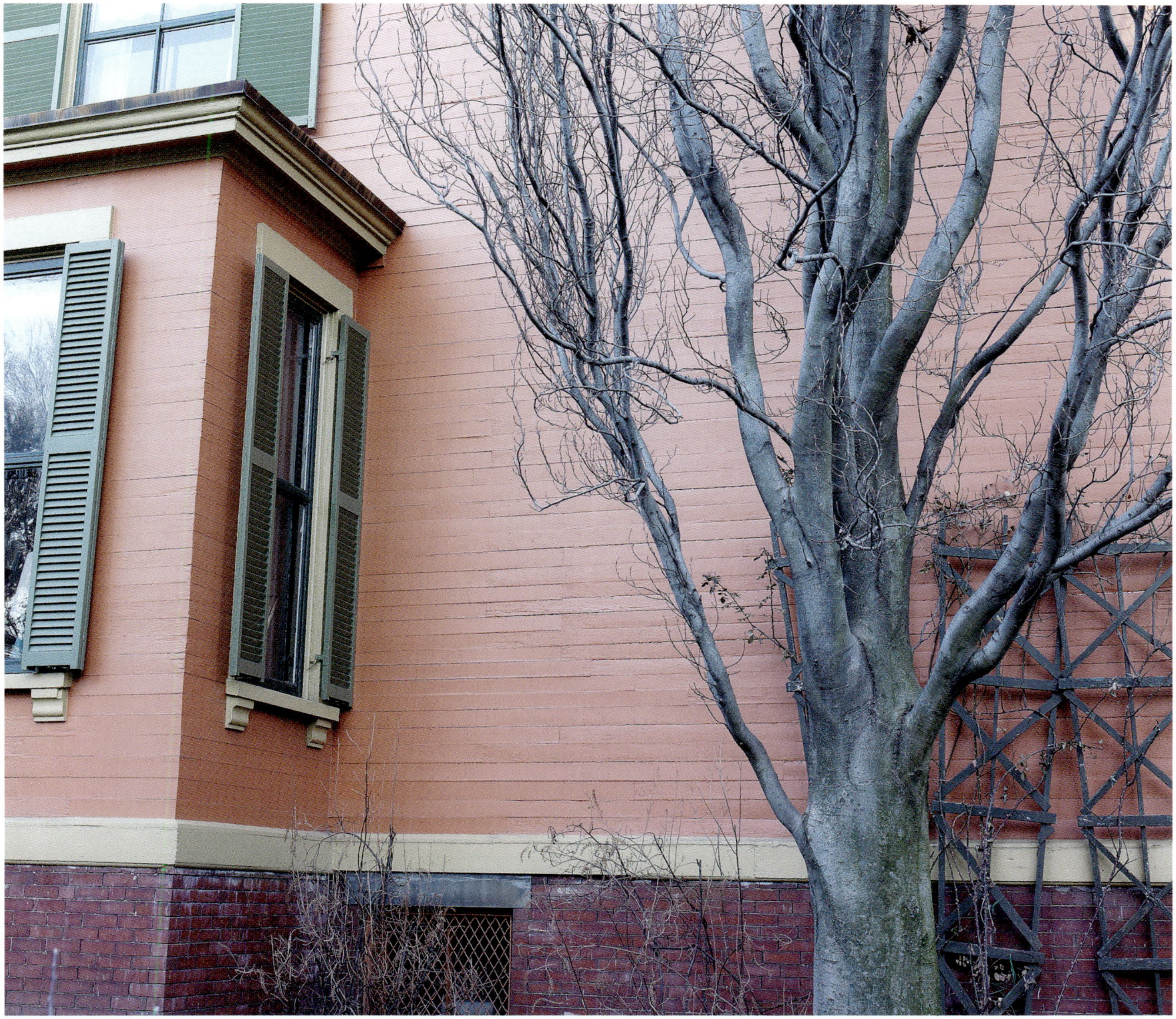

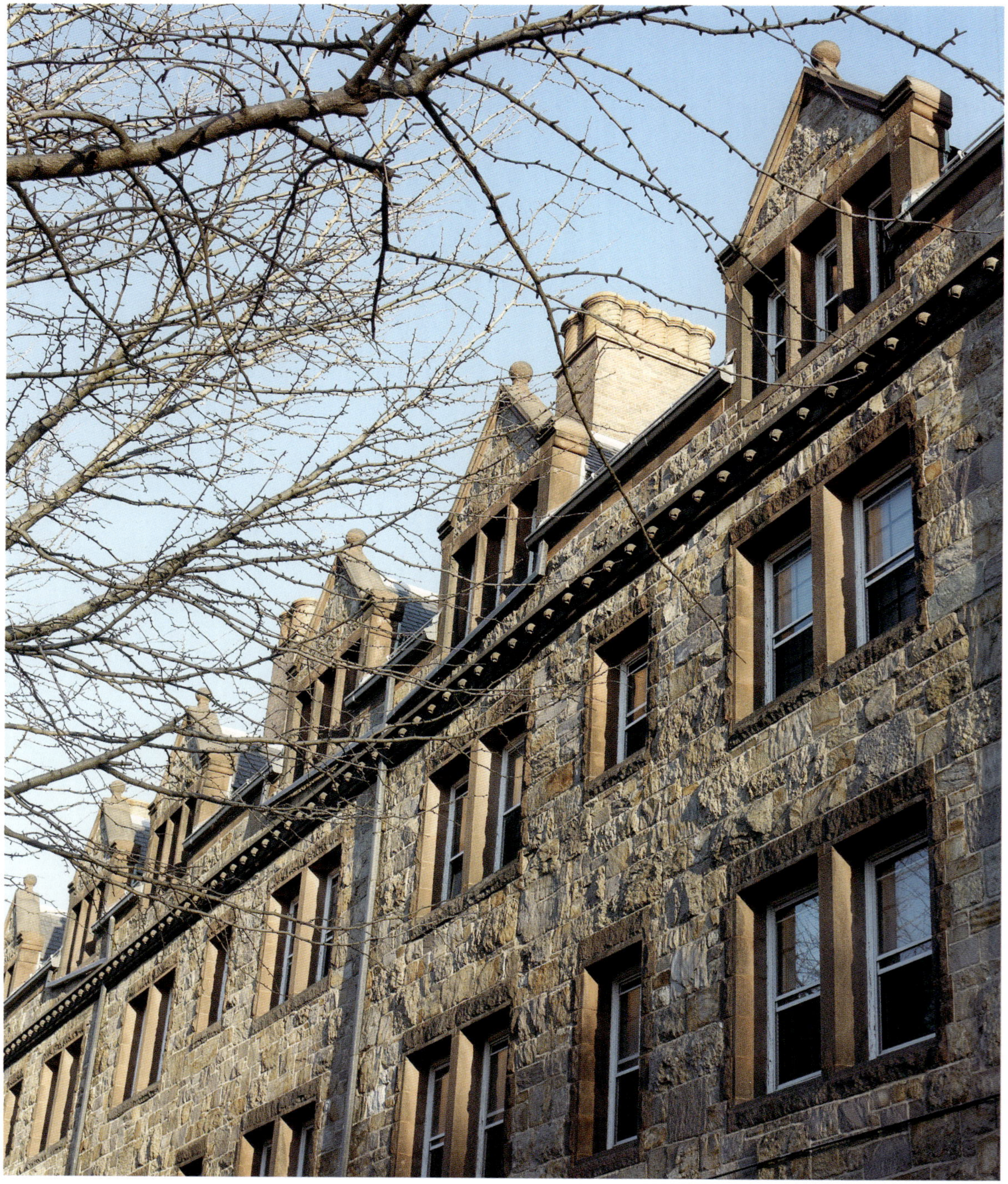

Cold Poached Nantucket Bay Scallops

Served with Baby Fennel Confit, Roasted Baby Beets, Quinoa, Blood Orange Vinaigrette, and Mache

Baby Fennel Confit
10 baby fennel
1 teaspoon coriander
1 teaspoon fennel seeds
1 teaspoon red pepper flakes
1 teaspoon mustard seeds
2 bay leaves
5 star anise
¾ gallon canola oil

Roasted Baby Beets
10 baby red beets
2 tablespoons canola oil
salt and pepper, to taste
1 shallot, sliced lengthwise
2 garlic cloves
6 sprigs thyme

Court Bouillon
2 onions
2 bunches of leeks
4 celery stalks
5 shallots
1 bottle white wine
1 gallon water
4 tablespoons salt
2 bay leaves
5 sprigs thyme
½ bunch parsley stems
1 tablespoon peppercorns

Scallops
2 pounds scallops, preferably Nantucket Bay scallops
court bouillon—recipe above

Toasted Quinoa
1 cup quinoa
2 cups water
salt and pepper, to taste
4 tablespoons chopped chervil
¼ cup olive oil

Blood Orange Vinaigrette
1 cup blood orange purée
2 shallots, minced
1 cup orange juice
½ cup red wine vinegar
2 egg yolks
salt to taste
2 cups grapeseed oil

Garnish
blood orange chip
mache

Serves 10

For the baby fennel confit, trim the bottoms of the fennel and wash them. Place in a heavy gauge pot, then add spices and cover with oil. Bring to the slightest simmer, just a lazy bubbling. Let simmer for approximately 1½-2 hours, until you can take a paring knife and easily cut into the fennel. Make sure to cut against the grain to increase resistance.

For the roasted baby beets, preheat oven to 350°. Trim tops off beets, leaving 1 inch of stem. Wash and dry. Heat a sauté pan in the oven. Add canola oil and beets and season with salt and pepper. Wait no more than 20 minutes, then check beets with a knife. The skin should be leathery and wrinkled. If it is, then add the shallot, garlic, and thyme and place pan back in oven for 5 minutes. Let beets cool, then rub them with a towel to remove skin. Trim tops off.

For the court bouillon, chop all the vegetables into medium dice. Put them in a large pot and add the wine, water and salt. Bring to a boil and simmer for 45 minutes. For the last 10 minutes, add bay leaves, thyme, parsley stems and peppercorns. Strain and cool.

For the scallops, remove the adductor muscles. Place scallops on bottom of heavy gauge pot. Cover them with court bouillon. Stir scallops with your hand in the pot with the heat set on high. When you cannot stand to keep your hand in the liquid, shut off the stove. Let the scallops sit for one minute, then remove them with a strainer. Cool them on a sheet pan with parchment, then store them in the liquid.

For the toasted quinoa, rinse the quinoa. Toast it in a dry sauté pan for about 5 minutes. Add water. Bring to a boil and reduce to a simmer. Let simmer for 15 minutes or until the germ comes from the grain. Spread quinoa on sheet tray to cool. Combine chervil and quinoa, then fold in olive oil and season with salt.

For the blood orange vinaigrette, combine blood orange purée and shallots in a saucepan over medium heat and reduce by ½. Add orange juice and reduce by ½. Remove from stove and add vinegar and egg yolks. Season, then whisk in grapeseed oil.

To assemble and serve, place fennel in the center of the plate, then surround it with the quinoa. Cascade the roasted baby beet over the top. Randomly place 8-10 scallops around plate as desired. Dress scallops with vinaigrette and also streak the plate. Garnish with blood orange chip and mache.

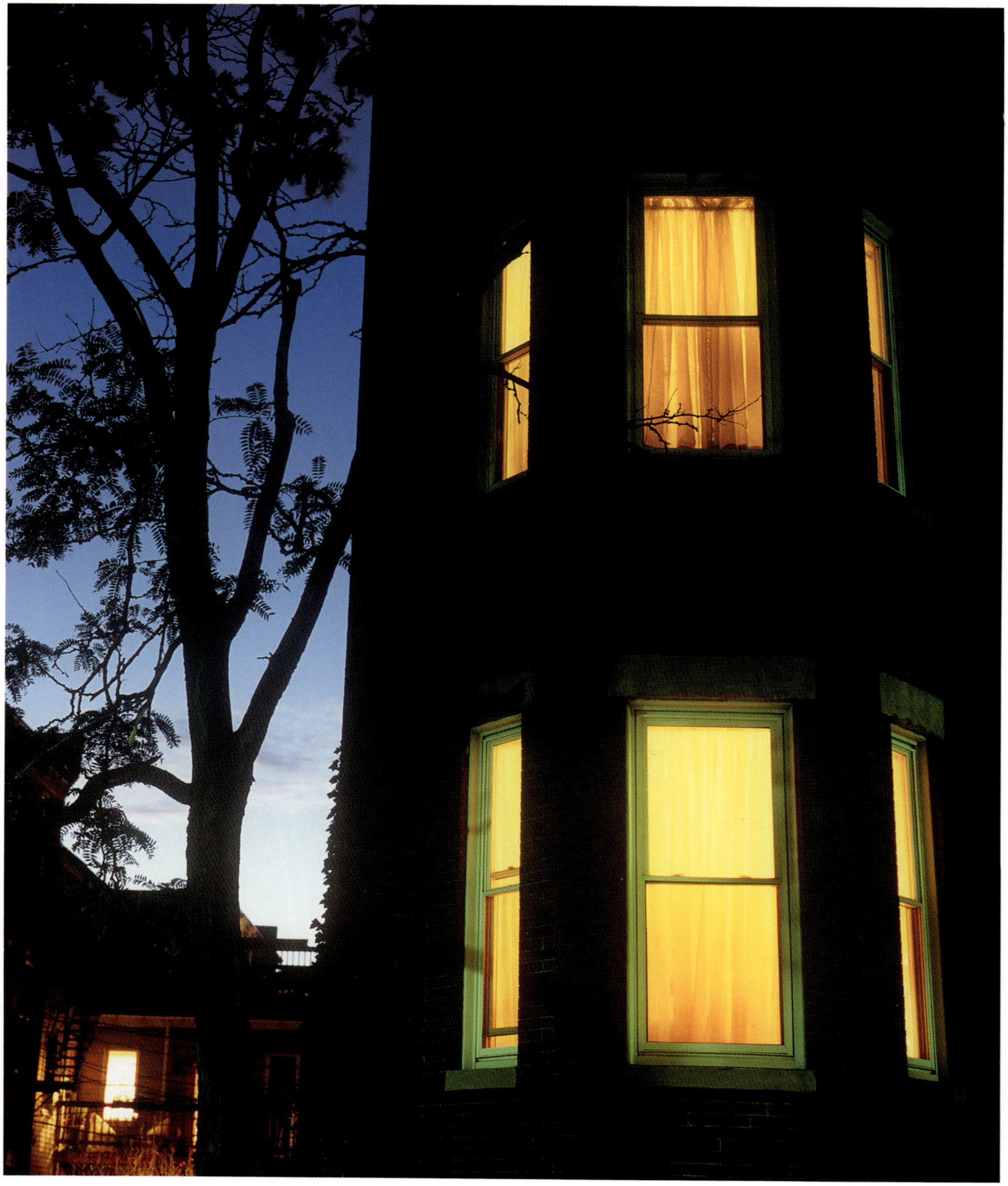

Brian Smestad
Denyce and Eric Rusch
Bob Saturley and Claudia Purves
George and Bernice Babinec
Bob and Alberta Saturley
Rena Gray
John and Leona Gray
Tosh Saturley
Graham, Anita, Conner, Alex, and Sean Saturley
Steve, Lydia, Alex and Tony Garrant
Jerry, Becky, Lily and Jack Gray
Jamie, Angie, and Jamison LaFleur
Brian Regan
Sean Haworth
David Evard
Lyn, Bill, Michelle and Kathryn Dubois
Gigi and Jones Andrews
Shelli, Michael, Sara, and Emily Powell
Adrian Roland Davis
Paul and Heather Stinson
Clyde, Debbie, and Tyler Cleveland
Greg Thatcher
Lawrence and Laurie Eyre
Jim Davis and Family
John and Brenda Narducci
Bill Teeple
Bob and Rebecca Hougher
Donna Colby
Doug Daller
Steve and Linda Dumont
Lukas Alonso
Bjorn Turnquist
Jeff Schick
Catherine Keenan
Stephanie Mitchell

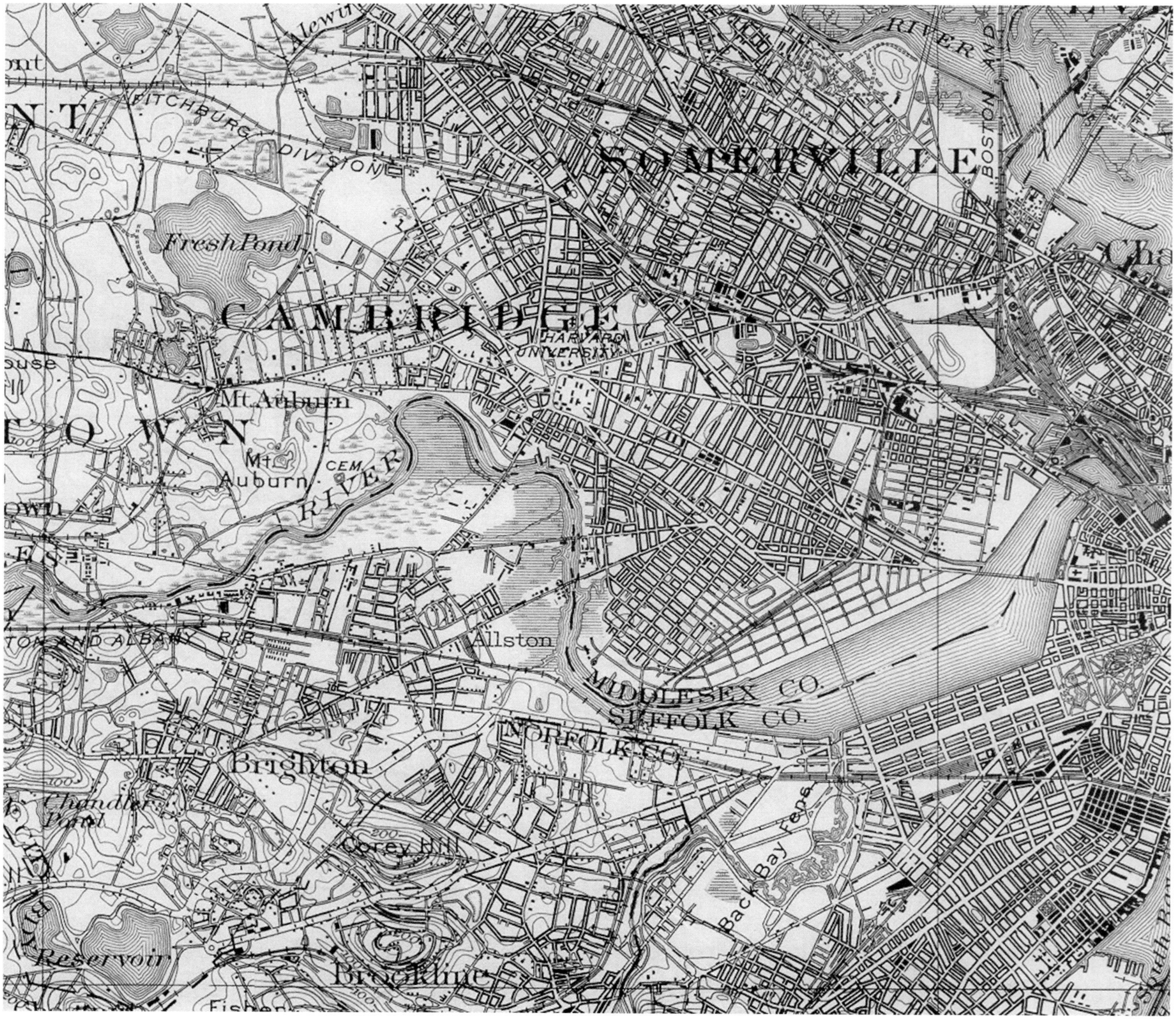
SOMERVILLE
CAMBRIDGE
HARVARD UNIVERSITY
FITCHBURG DIVISION
Fresh Pond
Mt. Auburn
Mt. Auburn
CEM.
RIVER
RIVER
Allston
MIDDLESEX CO.
SUFFOLK CO.
NORFOLK CO.
Brighton
Chandler Pond
Corey Hill
Reservoir
Brookline
Back Bay Fens

Casablanca 40 Brattle Street
Chez Henri 1 Shephard Street
Craigie Street Bistrot 5 Craigie Street
Finale 30 Dunster Street
Green Street 280 Green Street
Harvest 44 Brattle Street
L.A. Burdick 52 Brattle Street
OM Restaurant 92 Winthrop Street
Rialto 1 Bennett Street
Salts Restaurant 789 Main Street
Sandrine's Bistro 8 Holyoke Street
T.W. Foods 377 Walden Street
Temple Bar 1688 Massachusetts Avenue
The Blue Room One Kendall Square, Number 200
The Elephant Walk 2067 Massachusetts Avenue
Upstairs on the Square 91 Winthrop Street

chapter one

Spring

13

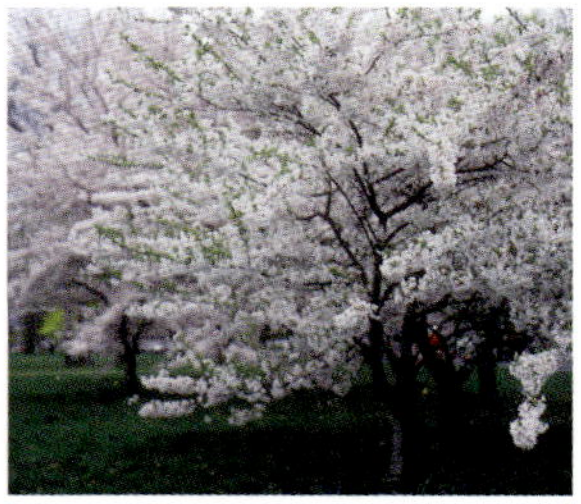

chapter two

Summer

41

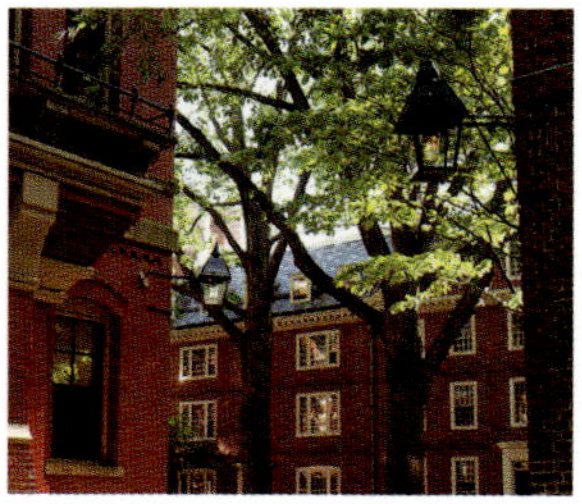

chapter three

Autumn

69

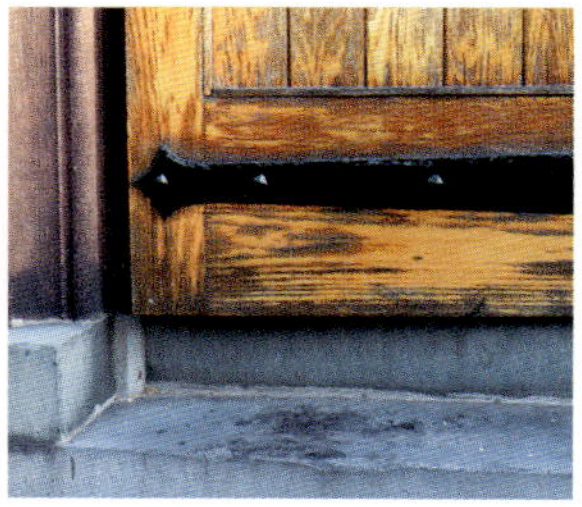

chapter four

Winter

97

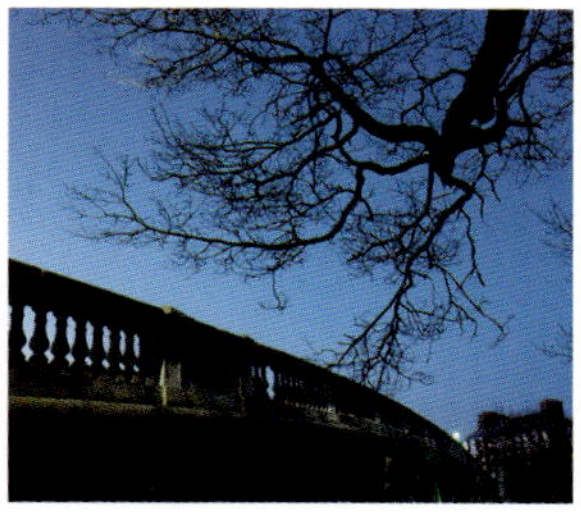